Effective vs. Efficient Computing

Edited by

FRED GRUENBERGER

Produced by

informatics inc®

Sherman Oaks, California 91401

PRENTICE-HALL, INC., *Englewood Cliffs, N.J.*

Library of Congress Cataloging in Publication Data
Main entry under title:

Effective vs. efficient computing.
    Proceedings of the 9th annual symposium sponsored
by Informatics Inc.; co-sponsored by the University of
California at Los Angeles and held on the Westwood
Campus March 22-24, 1972
    1. Electronic data processing--Congresses.
I. Gruenberger, Fred Joseph, ed. II. Informa-
tics Inc. III. California. University. University at
Los Angeles.
QA76. E33   001.6'4   73-4841
ISBN 0-13-246793-3

© 1973 by Prentice-Hall, Inc.

Englewood Cliffs, N. J.

Current printing (last digit):

10 9 8 7 6 5 4 3 2 1

PRENTICE-HALL INTERNATIONAL, INC., London
PRENTICE-HALL OF AUSTRALIA, PTY. LTD., Sydney
PRENTICE-HALL OF CANADA, LTD., Toronto
PRENTICE-HALL OF INDIA PRIVATE LIMITED, New Delhi
PRENTICE-HALL OF JAPAN, INC., Tokyo

CONTENTS

iii

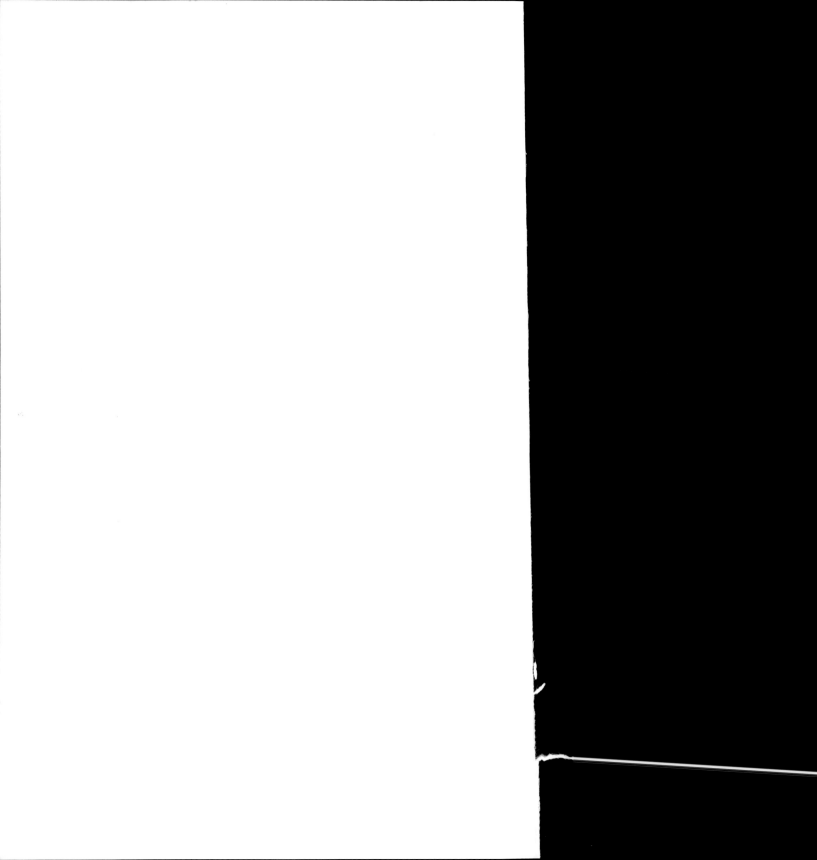

FOREWORD

In 1964, Informatics Inc. sponsored its first public computing symposium; the subject was Disk Files. Each year thereafter, there has been a symposium on a topic of current interest to the information processing community. The topic in 1965 was On-Line Computing Systems.

Starting in 1966, with the topic Computer Graphics, these symposia have been co-sponsored by the University of California at Los Angeles. Subsequent topics were:

1967: Computers and Communications — Toward a Computer Utility

1968: Critical Factors in Data Management

1969: Interactive Computers for Controlling Machines and Influencing People: Setting the Specifications for the Fourth Generation

1970: Expanding Use of Computers in the 70's: Markets — Needs — Technology

1971: Information Systems for Management

The papers collected in this volume constitute the proceedings of the ninth symposium, which was held on the Westwood Campus March 22-24, 1972. This is the sixth such set of papers published by Prentice-Hall, Inc.

The ninth symposium was attended by 140 representatives of industry, education, and government. Planning for the symposium began in mid-1971 with an advisory committee representing all three groups. The success of the symposium is largely due to the patient work of this committee.

Fred Gruenberger

PREFACE

EFFECTIVE vs. EFFICIENT COMPUTING

WALTER F. BAUER
President, Informatics Inc.

In the nine years that Informatics has sponsored an annual computing symposium, the emphasis has always been on selecting a topic of current general interest, usually to highlight a problem area of the field. The invited speakers are chosen for their expertise on that topic, plus their ability to present challenging and imaginative solutions. The topic for the 1972 symposium seemed to select itself. The planning committee was disturbed by the feeling that something was wrong with the way computers were being used. We are a long way from cost-effective use of computers, to be sure, but perhaps the time had come to examine the problem of computer utilization from a different viewpoint.

We do not mean to imply that the search for greater efficiency should be in any way attenuated. There is evidence that the time spent by many large computer installations in performing useful work (as opposed to red-tape operations involved in getting ready to do useful work) is less than 20% of the power-on time. But even discounting that fact, the resulting output is totally worthless if it is not effective. An unreadable printout, however efficiently it was produced, represents a waste of enormous amounts of money and, much worse, tremendous talent that is misdirected.

So the challenge to our speakers was presented as Effective versus Efficient computing, to which they responded with vigor. Each man has a unique point of view, but they all stayed close to the subject; namely, how effective have we been, and how can we become more effective? A panel of academicians considered a question that has arisen at many previous symposia: if we knew what to do, how could we go about arranging to have our formal training institutions produce the right type of person?

On the whole, the results of this exercise are surprisingly optimistic with positive indications of progress toward truly effective use of computers. It is part of the glory of computing that if anyone can show the right way in any application, then everyone is free to duplicate that procedure, with the comforting knowledge that the end result is feasible.

THE CHALLENGE OF DOING THE RIGHT THING

HERBERT R. J. GROSCH

Senior Staff Member
National Bureau of Standards

The most important artifact in our trade is the IBM Corporation. It is the dominant manufacturer and the most important single influence in our industry. The management of IBM has recently passed to Vin Learson, who is well known as a yachtsman. We, too, in the ranks of computer people, at least metaphorically speaking, have our yachts. We have done very well indeed in exploiting our new tool, the computer. But to paraphrase the title of a recent book about the stock market, Where are the customers' yachts? And where is society's yacht? There ought to be a vessel marked "Benefits of Data Processing" at least as big as the Queen Mary, painted in day-glow pink, flying the flag "Information is good for you." It is not clear to me that the customers' yachts or society's yacht are coming down the ways in the near future.

I take it as my task to state the problem: to seek ways that the customers and society can achieve the benefits that IBM, its officers, and most of us in the industry have already received. It's time that these benefits be shared with the people who have been paying the bills. That's what I think is involved in doing the right thing—in being effective.

It is, perhaps, a useful task also to direct attention to being efficient, but I will leave that task to others.

I should define some of my terms. By "manufacturer" I refer to those forces in our trade who produce hardware or software for the benefit or detriment of the others in the trade. The hardware part of the industry is, as I said, dominated by IBM, a company that some years back made 116% of the profit of the hardware side of the business; that's a fascinating statistic. There is as yet no single dominating company in the software industry. Both sides together are capable of continuing growth, worldwide, of 20% per year for the foreseeable future, black though that future may be for the customers and for society. So, by "manufacturer," I mean the hardware and software boys who are forcing the new technology on us.

By "us," I refer to the group that is euphemistically referred to as the profession. This is the group who have, until recently, made a very good living out of being the intermediaries between the manufacturers and those victims who pay the bill. We are that group and we have organized ourselves in curious ways into so-called professional societies to generate some very nice yacht capability. We are not all rich and we are certainly not all happy. We have fulfilled at least one of the requirements of the term "professional." We have not yet fulfilled the requirements of ethics or certification but we have managed to avoid taking directions from anyone.

When I refer to the "customers," I am not referring to those who install the hardware, write the programs, and manage the installations, but to the man upstairs who pays the bill. This is the airline, or the bank, or the governmental agency: the hopeful—ever hopeful—consumer of our product. This is the man who believes that if he keeps on investing in more and better hardware and software (and in us), 'way off in the distant future it will pay off in better operation and a happier circumstance for his business.

Three years ago, at this forum* I stated that I believed that things were going to get worse. I have put it in the form of Grosch's third Law: Things can get worse without limit. I predicted then the time of arrival of the fourth

---

*Grosch, H. R. J., "Are We Ready for Progress?" in Fourth Generation Computers: User Requirements and Transition, Prentice-Hall, 1970.

generation and underestimated somewhat the rapidity with which unbundling would appear on the scene, but I certainly was not wrong in stating that things would get worse. And I now state that they will continue to get worse, without limit.

So I have defined my view of manufacturer, user, and us. Users are a subclass of society as a whole. They function in that society and thus must concern themselves with the larger problems of society. All you have to do is look around at the lunar landscape of what might be a beautiful city here in Los Angeles to see some of the problems of our society—problems that our equipment and our expertise could help (and in some cases are trying to help). These problems, to be sure, are exacerbated by factors that are beyond our control, but they could be alleviated by systems that we do control.

The problems are not restricted to America. In my travels, I find similar problems in Europe, in Japan, and in the developing countries. Ours is not the only society that is influenced by the availability and the accomplishments of our technology. There are societies even hungrier than ours to be immersed in the wonders of computerization.

Eastern Europe is a good case in point. Yugoslavia, for which there are no restrictions on our export of high technology, is currently expanding its use of data processing by 100% per year. It has passed the point of having 250 machines; by the same time next year it will have between 400 and 600 machines, and most of these will be IBM. If we could persuade the Department of Defense to allow Bill Norris to ship Star-100's to Moscow in quantity, I am convinced that we would see detailed wall-to-wall planning in the Soviet Union. Such a move might, of course, put our own messier planning at risk, if it were not for the built-in safety factor; namely, that if DOD permitted the export of high-technology hardware, the Department of Commerce would insist that we ship our software with it. We are in no danger from the Soviet Union as long as they use our software as well as our hardware.

In all societies that seek to use computers there is a common parameter: the profit motive. Even in Eastern Europe there is a transformed variety of the profit parameter. Out of charity it is called the profit motive; it could be called an uglier, more down-to-earth (and, in my opinion, more realistic) term: greed. Whatever you call it, it exists throughout the world; everyone wants to make a buck, or the social equivalent thereof. Up and down the world, the tool that we have somewhat mastered is used primarily as a means of gaining power. Only secondarily, and almost accidentally, is it used for those things that we seek as human beings--as individuals. The social benefits to be gained from the use of computers are far down on the list of organizational objectives.

I would not want to be thought of as attacking the computing industry. Recall my remark about the lunar landscape. Let me remind you also of a recent pronouncement by Ed David, the President's science advisor, who is at least a corresponding member of our profession, to the effect that safety and pollution prevention are too expensive for automobiles; that it's simply cheaper to die or to suffocate. It isn't only computer manufacturers, computer organizations, and computer users who are stinkers.

Let me turn now to the total costs of doing business, not only in the computing industry, and not only in this country. There are, I think, seven major components of costs.

1. Material costs. On the hardware side of our business this includes basic components, such as the transistors and the copper wires, plus plant facilities to bring all the components together. Even in the esoteric discipline called software manufacture, there are material costs of pencils and paper and reels of magnetic tape.

2. People costs. This is the cost of labor: salaries, commissions, fees, and hourly wages—these make up a second, well-recognized cost.

3. Capital. This is a dominant factor in this country and a transformed factor in other countries. To put together an organization of production, whether in Los Angeles, or New Zealand, or Moscow, you have to commit a significant investment.

4. Customer relations. This is only now emerging, in this country, as a major cost of doing business: to maintain warranties, to replace defective products, and to insure customer satisfaction over and above the traditional stance of caveat emptor.

5. New knowledge. This is a cost that applies particularly to our business. It is not possible to stand still in any business, but for us it is not possible to wait for someone else to develop the new knowledge that is needed to advance and to compete. Other industries, such as mass transportation, can hope for a fallout from aerospace, but in computing we must arrange to generate the new techniques ourselves. We have done an outstanding job in this area in componentry and a good job, at least in the early days, in software. For our industry, this cost has been one of the largest portions of the total.

6. Physical environment. This is the cost of preventing pollution, which is now becoming a major cost for some industries. It is of only minor concern to us, since there is little that our industry does that directly dirties up the environment in which we operate.

7. Social costs. These are usually labeled, pejoratively, taxes. They include the cost of education and training, not only of the people who are to replace us, but of the consumers who must be trained to use up the goodies that we produce. Social costs should be welcomed. Instead, they are resisted, at least in this country.

Now, any organization must arrange to apportion those seven costs, whether the organization be a profit-making venture, a university, a governmental organization, or even a nonprofit group. The cost assigned to the end product must be optimized as a function of those seven input costs. It is not proper, in my opinion, to optimize the organizational procedures only with regard to payment for the use of capital. The young people in this country and in some others have seen very clearly that profit alone is not acceptable.

In our trade, profitability is a managed item. We have a special situation, because IBM essentially is able to "Yo-Yo" the profits any way it chooses, at least in the hardware and nearby parts of our business. A gross of 8 billion a year; profits of 2 billion a year; profits after taxes of 1 billion a year--this gives them the power not only to manipulate the customer, but, to an increasing extent, to manipulate society. The prospects of competition, of regulation, or of nationalization are, in my view, zero. The IBM Corporation may become the largest and most powerful company in the free world. I believe that by the end of this decade, all its present competitors will have disappeared, all over the world. Indeed, I have made up a timetable for this course of events, which starts with XDS in this country, and ends with the last of the foreign competitors, the combine of Fujitsu and Hitachi in Japan.

In this environment, we (the profession) must give special attention to the question of whether we are doing the right thing. Competition, the touchstone of old-fashioned capitalism, is not going to do it for us. I will cite some examples to support this pessimistic (but, I think, inspirational) view of our responsibilities.

First, let us consider some of the "successes" of our trade, most of which, it seems to me, have been of very dubious social value. In the zero'th generation—the generation of punched card and electromechanical devices prior to electronics—one of the outstanding successes was the calculations that produced the atomic bomb. At Los Alamos, computational work was done on equipment that ran at the rate of a thousand operations per hour, doing the shock wave analysis on the inside of an almost unimaginable device and bringing it to fruition.

We moved up into the first generation: the ENIAC, the SSEC, the early IBM electronic calculators, and then the IBM 700 series and the Remington 1100 series, not to overlook the overseas counterparts like LEO. What did we do with those machines? We designed tin airplanes and missiles. Sure, I'd rather fly around in a 707 than a DC-3, but I got a lot more attention in the DC-3, and it's not at all clear just how much we've advanced.

The second generation was marked by transistorization, pioneered by Philco. With this new breed, we designed Rickover's submarines.

I'll tell you: on dubious social projects, we do just fine.

And what of the third generation, which burst upon us in 1964, marked by integrated circuits and operating systems? What have we done with that? It's a nice question. I think that one of the most dubious of all achievements that can be claimed in computing is the creation of OS/360--a traveling catastrophe of unimaginable magnitude. It is more dangerous in some respects, at least to our intellectual welfare, than atomic weapons, missiles, or the 747.

So here we are in the fourth generation (for nearly two years now), which is the harbinger of still more atrocities along the lines of invasion of privacy, civil rights, and domination of our law processes by centralized FBI-type agencies. Indeed, the forces of dubious value in our society are making great use of computers.

Most of us would like to do other things with computers: put out payrolls cheaper; manage magazine subscriptions more effectively; keep the books for a department store more humanely; calculate credit card accounts correctly and lower the charges for them rather than raise them. What have we done with all our computer power and our new sophistication in these areas?

I just got back from viewing the Star-100 in Minneapolis, where the first copy is being readied for Livermore, and copy number two is being made for a less dubious—but still dubious—purpose; namely, the General Motors Research Center, where they will use it to design curlier fenders for us lucky drivers. That machine, suitably pipelined, is capable of performing one hundred million multiplications per second.

I go back to the minus first generation, when the combined computing unit was a desk calculator and me, and the best that one could achieve was a hundred operations per hour. Between those two points in time—from the key-driven operations of thirty years ago to the Star—we have an increase in speed of a factor of 3.6 billion. Even following Grosch's law, the increase in efficiency should be around the square root of that figure, which is a factor of 60,000. If we consider a unit of payroll calculation that cost a dollar in the 30's, we ought to be able to do the same work today for 1/600 of a cent. (Or, on lesser machines than the Star-100, which is not particularly suited to payroll calculations, for perhaps 1/100 of a cent.) I hardly need to point out that we can't do this.

My old desk calculator had storage capacity equivalent to 100 bits. I recently saw computing equipment at Fort Mead, intended for management purposes, in which one component had storage capacity of 3×10^{12} bits. There are commercial storage devices now available for 10^{12} bits at a million dollars or so each. So our storage capacity has gone up in the same time period by a factor of thirty billion.

Again, for contrast, operations with a desk calculator tend toward about one discoverable mistake per hour due to operator error. Today we expect to run large systems for 100 hours or more between detectable machine errors. All told, then, we've gone up by nearly 4 billion in speed, 30 billion in capacity, and at least ten times in reliability what we were when I started out. And with all that, we not only don't do payroll as cheaply as these factors would indicate; we don't do anything. Murray Laver, speaking at this same symposium three years ago, accounted for it by saying that our systems are all silted up with software. What we have done is share the wealth—the vastly increased computing power—with the users. We gave them some of it, but we retained most of it for ourselves, to drive those layers of software.

To return to my metaphor of the yachts, one element in our yacht is the freedom to burn up the speed and memory capacity we have, for our own ends. What it amounts to, is that we selfishly and wastefully misuse our tools for our own edification, our own glorification, and simply to have fun, rather than to furnish better and cheaper computing to our customers. We see the same thing in the medical and legal fields: a tendency to operate the systems for the benefit of those who are in them, rather than the ultimate consumers, or for society as a whole.

We are at a time of economic reconsideration or, if you prefer, a depression. Even so, many parts of our economy

are free of external examination, and data processing is one
of those parts. It is true that defective or misapplied machines do get shipped back. It is true that companies do go
bankrupt due to bad bookkeeping, poor forecasting, or over-
expensive computer installations. But the overall effect is
not to question the necessity of using the computer. There
is seldom any question raised about our professionalism.
Rather, the failures are taken to imply a need for more powerful equipment and more sophisticated software. I claim
that effective as well as efficient use of the computer com-
pels us to think, over and over, for whose benefit we wish
to operate. At our lower level of organizational responsibility, we should share all seven of the costs that I listed.
We should concern ourselves frequently and with careful
consideration with the other costs of the management of
large organizations, rather than being concerned only with
our own professional pride and the short-term profits—
which are often the long-term detriment—of the organization within society.

I don't believe that we are at a useful turning point yet.
The young people are not about to remake our society, nor
are we going to switch from capitalism to socialism. We
are not about to see a balancing of those seven costs, outside our trade. But within our trade, we have an opportunity to suboptimize. We could demonstrate for our organizational superiors the long-term desirability of trading some
of that speed and capacity in favor of organizational good,
customer effectiveness, and social effectiveness, rather
than keeping it for ourselves to play games with our multi-
layered software systems.

There are four things we could do in setting up new projects or in reconsidering or abandoning old projects. First
of all, we should make sure that the goal is clear, rather
than merely deciding that something would be fun to do, or
challenging to try, or would make a good paper for the ACM
publications. For instance, what is the goal of operating an
efficient airlines reservation system? Is it to attract more
customers for the airline? Is it to provide wheelchairs,
baby carriages, and kosher meals? Is it to reduce the costs
of day-to-day operations? The goal should be spelled out

and agreed to, not only by us, but by the customer.

At this stage of the game, it would be worthwhile to consider society's values, too. For example (speaking personally, now, and not as an employee of the Department of Commerce, or as an ACM Council member), I think it would be undesirable to contribute to the further expansion of advertising in this country. If I were asked to aid in the development of new hardware or software to increase the power of advertising, I would flatly refuse. Not everyone would agree with me on that. All I urge is that you think about it, and decide for yourself whether or not what you are asked to do is worthwhile.

After you have a defined goal, and you have decided that you wish to pursue it, then you need a metric to measure progress toward that goal. You need a quantitative measure, even if it is good to only one-half or one significant digit. And we don't have such measures now. It is a serious matter that we are unable to compare two hardware/software/people combinations in any depth to determine which is more effective.

My first goal, when I joined the Bureau of Standards, was to establish means of measuring computing capability. When I left the directorship, after three years, I had not moved 1% toward success in that area, and my successor has not been able to do much better. It is a matter that the profession has not supported and the customer has not heard about. The vendors, from IBM through the dwarfs and down to the mini-dwarfs, do not want it to happen. Every manufacturer wants his installations to be as inefficient as possible, subject only to the restriction that they not be so inefficient that they are replaced by equipment from another manufacturer. And that is why standards and performance measurements are very poorly supported, in this country and abroad.

But even if we can establish some metrics, we should also consider, in our own organizations, methods and the desirability of passing the benefits of what we have learned on to other people. This could range from mundane things like patent rights for software; such topics could be the subjects of whole symposia. We all wish to stand on the shoulders of others and must, in turn, permit others to stand on our shoulders. Methods for doing this are well established but not honored, except in the academic world, where the "publish or perish" syndrome forces it. In the industrial world, we tend to keep our knowledge to ourselves, because the profit syndrome says that that's the way to make more profit. I'm not talking about trading software; I'm talking about trading skills and attitudes and broad experiences. There is no reason why the same mistakes should be repeated endlessly.

So I believe that if you work for those four things—define the goals; decide for yourself that they are worth working for; establish metrics; and arrange to communicate new knowledge to others—then you will have gone a long way toward establishing effective as well as efficient computing.

ASSESSING RETURNS FROM THE
DATA PROCESSING INVESTMENT

EPHRAIM R. McLEAN

Assistant Professor of
Information Systems
Graduate School of Management
University of California
Los Angeles, California

In the field of data processing, the last decade has been characterized by a mood of unbridled optimism. In the face of unrealized expectations, managers have repeatedly buried their failures—or worse, learned to live with them—and then turned to even more ambitious undertakings with hardly a pause. While other aspects of corporate activity were subject to hard-headed scrutiny, the computer budget appeared to be sacred. Its mystique allowed it to escape the careful review that other expenditures had to undergo. The tight coterie of computer specialists talked in terms of microsecond cycle times and megabyte memories with very little concern as to the purposes to which this impressive technology was being applied.

Fortunately, this era seems to have come to an end, and many managers are beginning to ask some long-overdue questions, most of which can be reduced to a single fundamental one: are we doing the right thing or merely doing the thing right?

Effectiveness vs. Efficiency

In a jocular way, this question gets at the heart of the difference between two frequently encountered words — effectiveness and efficiency. These two terms are often erroneously used interchangeably. Failure to distinguish between them goes far beyond mere niceties of English usage; it can lead to misdirected effort and inappropriate attention. Effectiveness is, after all, "doing the right thing," while efficiency is "doing the thing right."

Efficiency, as defined through long usage in the field of engineering, is a measure of a unit of output in terms of a unit of input. More particularly, in computing it can be defined as "the ratio of time spent on useful work to total power-on time.[1] In this sense, "useful work" means that time which is not idle or used for reruns, restarts, maintenance, or other nonproductive activity. Whether, in fact, this computer work is really useful — from a managerial standpoint — is quite another matter. This is much more difficult to judge but is a far more critical issue.

From the preceding, it should not be implied that efficiency is not an important concern; it is. It is a necessary, but not sufficient, condition for success. As an aside, it should be pointed out that companies are not doing very well even on the efficiency dimension. In a recent study of 155 computer centers by A. T. Kearney and Co., they found that "only 48 percent of available computer time is used productively."[2] The study went on to say that if these findings were typical of all computer centers (and there is no reason to believe they would not be), this represents an annual waste of $3.5 billion in computer time.

If efficiency is directed toward the conversion of inputs into outputs with the smallest amount of loss, what then is

---

1. Fred Gruenberger, "Problems and Priorities," Datamation, Vol. 18, No. 3, March 1972, p. 49.

2. As reported in the Communications of the ACM, Vol. 14, No. 2, February 1971, p. 133.

effectiveness, or doing the "right" thing? For one, it is not, as so often happens, the EDP staff doing its "own" thing. This brings to mind the distinction which is sometimes made between computer "closed shop" and "open shop" operation. In a closed shop, the EDP staff has firm control over all programming and use of the computer, with the result that very elegant programs with tightly written code are produced— but focusing on the wrong problems. In an open shop, the programs are likely to be hastily written and inefficient to run; but they are dealing with the problems that are of most concern to management.

How then do we define what is the "right" thing? There is no absolute answer; it must be drawn from the context in which the EDP group finds itself. In other words, the determination of what is right depends upon the organization. Unless a computer center is a totally independent entity (as is the case with a computer service bureau), it must function as a part of a larger organization. And this larger organization will typically have goals and objectives that are far removed from the usual concerns of EDP specialists.

Ideally, it is hoped that all parts of an organization will have objectives that are consistent with those of the organization as a whole. This is known as "goal congruence." To the extent that there is a lack of goal congruence, the system is said to be dysfunctional. Unfortunately, there has been a fair amount of what might be called organizationally dysfunctional behavior on the part of many EDP professionals. The goals which they pursue are more related to professional fulfillment than to the frequently unexciting tasks of programming a report or designing a file for a production manager.

Just as one can have no quarrel with a concern for efficiency, neither should one fault the growing desire on the part of many EDP experts for increased professionalism. This is necessary and desirable; but as with efficiency, it should not be an end in itself. The true professional can uphold the finest tenets of his craft while still pursuing the objectives of the organization of which he is a part. The example earlier of the contrast between closed and open shop was, of course, much too simple minded. There is no reason why computer programs and systems cannot be both efficient and yet directed at the critical problems of the enterprise. Too often, however, a programmer will dwell on a problem because it is "technically interesting" or a systems analyst will recommend a new application because it is an "advancement of the state of the art" without sufficient consideration of the impact of such actions upon the overall corporate objectives.

The Type III Error

In the field of statistics, there is much attention devoted to the two types of errors which can be made in testing a hypothesis. A Type I Error is that which occurs when a true hypothesis is rejected; a Type II Error occurs when a false hypothesis is accepted. John Tukey has suggested that an even greater source of error is testing the wrong hypothesis; what might be called the Type III Error. [3]

This analogy is an appropriate one here. Testing the wrong hypothesis or, more simply, attacking the wrong problem is an all-too-frequent occurrence. Therefore, a watchword for management might well be: avoid the Type III Error. To this we might add the possibility of a Type IV Error. According to Howard Raiffa, this is the solving of the right problem—too late. [4] Of course, it would be desirable to avoid all classes of error; but this is not always possible. It should be clear, however, that the latter two are far more dangerous than the first two.

A Management Crisis

The extent of the growth of EDP expenditures over the last decade has finally begun to be realized. But the exact dimensions of this growth are still unclear. Some companies have found that their computer budgets have increased inexorably over the years, quite independent of their overall growth. Through good years and bad, through increasing sales and

---

3. Howard Raiffa, Decision Analysis, Reading, Mass: Addison-Wesley, 1968, p. 264.

4. Ibid.

decreasing sales, the computer budget goes up.

What is perhaps even more alarming is the experience of one company that graphed its sales figures and computer expenses over the last several years and then attempted to fit a curve through each of these sets of points. Reassuringly, the sales figures were increasing in a uniform, straight-line fashion. The computer costs were also increasing, but here an exponential curve provided a much better fit than the use of a linear curve such as was used for the sales. The implication was clear; in a very few years, the costs of EDP would, if unchecked, exceed the total revenues of the company!

This revelation did not result in a wholesale across-the-board cut; that would have been the worst thing that could have been done. It did, however, force the company to examine much more closely what it was getting for its money. And this was a company that had prided itself on its very careful, and conservative, approach to EDP investment analysis.

In many other companies, there is simply no attempt made to measure the benefits—or lack of benefits—that are resulting from their EDP expenditures. Studies made by both McKinsey and Company[5] and Booz, Allen and Hamilton over the last several years have found that, with a few notable exceptions, most companies have a very poor idea of the benefits that are accruing from their use of computers and where it is they should look for future applications. It should not be implied that to undertake this needed measurement is an easy task; it is not. But even attempting to measure can be a tremendous step in the right direction. Only in this way can both corporate management and EDP management bring to bear the attention needed in this critical area.

Naturally, it is a source of concern when companies spend a great deal of money with little idea of the corresponding benefits. It is a far more serious matter, however, when companies make no attempt to measure the cost side of the

5. See, for instance, "Unlocking the Computer's Profit Potential," The McKinsey Quarterly, Fall, 1968, pp. 17-31.

equation. With computers proliferating and staffs expanding, with each division wanting its own computer center because of its own specialized needs, and with each computer center arguing for the replacement of equipment which is barely two or three years old, it is small wonder that the corporation as a whole is hard pressed to keep an accurate count of the total cost. And what of the indirect costs: staff studies, involvement of operating personnel, dual systems during conversion, and opportunity costs, to name a few? It is possible that these may approach in size the direct computer expenditures.

While acknowledging the difficulty of the task, we should not let this serve as an excuse for failing to make the attempt. Recently, a billion-dollar corporation which experienced rapid growth during the sixties belatedly began taking a careful look at its total EDP costs. "We had no idea of how much we were spending on computerized systems," a corporate executive admitted privately. "Let's face it; when you have plenty of money in the bank, who bothers to balance the checkbook?"

In this effort to measure costs and benefits, computer professionals are frequently of little help. As with the confusion between effectiveness and efficiency, there is a confusion between accuracy and precision.

Precision is a function of the fineness of measure, and computer programmers will frequently go to "double precision" arithmetic in order to obtain an answer with more significant digits. Accuracy, on the other hand, is a measure of correctness or freedom from error. Thus, a figure with only two or three significant digits may be a far more accurate representation of some real-world entity than a highly precise ten-digit number which is grossly in error because of a failure to take into account some key information.

Unfortunately, EDP experts are typically more comfortable with problems of precision than with those of accuracy. Computers are renowned for generating reams of print-outs and countless columns of numbers. The question which must be answered is whether or not these numbers are telling the whole story, or even a true story. It is perhaps a little like

Oscar Wilde's cynic "who knows the price of everything and the value of nothing."

Some Benefits of EDP

What then of the benefits management should be receiving? As mentioned earlier, the answer must be found in terms of the organization of which the EDP group is a part. The EDP efforts must be consistent with, and in support of, corporate management's goals and objectives. Naturally, different organizations will have different objectives, so no detailed prescription can be given; but the functions of management are fairly universal across a wide range of organizations, even though each may have differing aims and structures.

Many definitions of management have been given over the years, with each one dependent to some extent upon the particular point the author is trying to make. This paper is no different. For my purposes, I shall define the process of management as the acquisition and utilization of resources (broadly defined) in the pursuit of organization goals. Therefore, in order to be considered a success, EDP activities must support this managerial task—that is, the effective use of resources. And what is meant by resources? Most simply, they are

- materials

- equipment and facilities

- capital

- and, most importantly, people.

In the following discussion, a number of examples are given to illustrate how the above-mentioned resources can be used more effectively. These examples should not be considered definitive or exhaustive in any way. Rather, they are merely suggestive of the range of potential benefits that may accrue through the application of computers to corporate activities.

Materials

Among those organizations which produce a product (as

distinct from offering a service), the acquisition, conversion, and sale of materials comprise a central corporate
activity. The following are representative examples of areas in which improvements have been realized by a number
of companies.

Improved Purchasing. The use of automatic reordering
systems, the pooling of requirements across several divisions or departments, the advantages of volume buying and
the use of economic order quantities, and the ability to forecast requirements and anticipate material needs are all aid-
ed by well-designed EDP systems. In the latter case, the
use of computer models to help predict price fluctuations in
the commodity markets has been particularly helpful to trad-
er and end-user alike. To help improve vendor selection,
systems have been devised to allow detailed analysis of vendors' past performances on such things as price, delivery,
and quality.

Inventory Control. For raw, in-process, and finished
goods inventories, a number of benefits have been realized
through computer-based inventory control systems. Faster
turnovers have been achieved, and losses due to spoilage
and obsolescence have been reduced by instituting tighter
controls which are made possible by the computer.

Marketing. Here there is a wide spectrum of systems
ranging from simple reports giving sales statistics to very
complicated sales forecasting techniques and models of consumer behavior. Indeed, the whole field of market research
has benefited greatly from its recognition of the potential
contribution of the computer. However, given the highly
competitive nature of marketers, the more successful a computer application is likely to be, the less likely an outsider
will hear about it.

Equipment and Facilities

In the area of equipment and facilities, the benefits are
less obvious; yet in many instances they can yield substantial results.

Equipment and Utilization. In capital-intensive industries,
the increased utilization of expensive equipment can lead to

significant operating economies. By increasing the percentage of capacity at which such things as machine tools are operating, production can be expanded markedly without a
corresponding increase in the number of machines. This
could eliminate the need to spend hundreds of thousands of
dollars on additional equipment. For the railroads, an increased freight car utilization of a few percentage points
could result in millions of dollars of savings—a major reason for the railroads' recent interest in computers.

The computer can contribute to this increased machine
utilization in a number of ways. By improved scheduling
techniques, fewer set-ups and changeovers are necessary;
and those changeovers that do occur can be simplified by a
determination of optimal tooling sequences. This will also
lead to longer production runs and larger lot sizes. Maintenance too should be improved with the help of the computer.
In fact, Mobil Oil has developed a major industrial marketing strategy around its offering to its customers of a computer-based M.I.S., in this case a Maintenance Information
System.

Space and Facilities. In addition to the advantages cited
above for better inventory control, another benefit is that of
reduced space requirements. Through the use of a well-
designed inventory system, one company not only avoided
the need to build an additional warehouse, but also eliminated
costly temporary storage costs which occurred every summer before the annual plant shutdown. Demurrage is another
storage cost which can be reduced through more careful planning and scheduling. Finally, this same planning and scheduling system can give business a marketing advantage where
lead-times are reduced and firm delivery schedules can be
promised with greater confidence.

Capital

As many a corporate executive has realized during the
crunch of the last few years, "money matters." And substantial strides have been made in reducing interest and
carrying costs, in applying cash management techniques,
and in improving credit and loss experience.

Interest Costs. For some reason, the costs of providing capital to meet the needs of the business are often overlooked when new projects are undertaken. For example, in the earlier reference to the use of the computer in improved purchasing efforts, the assurances that no discounts will be lost because of late payments and, more recently, that bills are not paid too early, i. e. , before they are due, are instances of ways of avoiding interest costs.

Also, the costs of carrying large accounts receivables can be substantial. Upon undertaking a systems study recently, one organization found that its average account was sixty days old and that total receivables were in excess of three million dollars. By streamlining the billing procedures, with the computer playing a central role, this amount was cut almost in half, with an annual saving of nearly a hundred thousand dollars (the exact amount being dependent upon the current cost of short-term borrowing). Parenthetically, the study had been undertaken primarily in hopes that two or three billing clerks could be eliminated (they were).

Returning to the inventory control example, in addition to the benefits already cited, the interest costs of carrying excessive inventories and of the space to hold them should not be overlooked when calculating savings.

Cash Management. Rarely have astute financial managers been as valued as they have been in the last few years. With interest rates hitting their highest levels in nearly a century, the financial vice president or controller who was able to weather this storm was a valuable individual indeed.

In order to keep bank balances to an absolute minimum, managers are exploring a number of ways to release idle funds. Westinghouse has a sophisticated system which allows the company to adjust its balances at the various banks around the country in which it has accounts so that no one bank has more funds than necessary. Other companies are becoming very skillful at playing the "float." Of course, a computer is not always at the center of these activities; but frequently it does figure prominently.

Credit and Losses. Many lending institutions have turned to the computer to assist them in maintaining credit records and in running credit checks. (Indeed, more than one critic has spoken out against the loss of privacy which can accompany the creation and maintenance of such files.) Without the computer, the growth of credit services such as Bank-Americard and Master Charge would have been impossible. Improved loss experience, while difficult to measure accurately, is nevertheless quite real. The Pacific Bell System recently reported significant reductions in their losses due to the fraudulent use of telephone credit cards. Although naturally reluctant to give any details of their new system, Bell did admit that it was "computer-based."

People

For a long time, the most commonly used justification for the installation of computers was personnel reduction; however, this has just about come to an end. The time when substantial savings could be made from widespread job eliminations has passed; most of these applications have already been realized, and the remaining potential is fairly small. On the other hand, although it is increasingly difficult to cut payrolls, the computer is still making inroads in lessening the growth in employment from what might have occurred if the computer had not been involved. Many companies, in particular those in the insurance industry, have reported large increases in sales volumes while, with the help of the computer, the sizes of their clerical staffs have been held nearly constant. In appraising benefits, it is just as important to account for what has not happened, i.e., a growth in the size of the labor force, as it is to measure what has happened, i.e., a net reduction in payroll costs.

As service industries are expanding more rapidly than other parts of the economy, it is this second benefit—that of allowing people to work more effectively—that offers the greatest promise for the future. And this benefit should extend throughout the entire organization: hourly worker, clerical worker, and management alike.

Factory productivity can begin climbing again; clerks can process more transactions; salesmen can make more sales; and, hopefully, managers can make better decisions. Which brings us back again to the point made earlier; namely, the ultimate success of the EDP effort must be measured in terms of supporting the management process.

No attempt will be made here to explore the much-vaunted total management information system. The possibility of a chief executive officer sitting in his office and, with the help of a computer terminal, building a model to help him decide where his firm should be five years in the future is still fairly remote. So is the total "corporate data base" in which any manager can ask any question concerning the functioning of the enterprise and get an instant response. However, there are signs that more modest versions of these systems are beginning to be constructed—and with the solid endorsement of top management. In any event, the pros and cons of such efforts have been discussed at much greater length elsewhere.[6]

Obtaining Success

It is one thing to recommend the design of computer systems to support management decision making; it is quite another thing to achieve it. If a new system is perceived as the private domain of the EDP specialists and not of the organization as a whole, its chances of success are far smaller than they might otherwise be.

The phrase "user-oriented system" is frequently encountered; unfortunately, it is often little more than empty words. Management does not understand the importance of its role in the design and implementation process, and the computer specialists are loath to yield any of their perceived prerogatives. All too often the user is forced to adapt to the system

---

6. John Dearden, "Myth of Real-Time Management Information," Harvard Business Review, Vol. 44, No. 3, May-June 1966, pp. 123-132.

Robert V. Head, "Real-Time Management Information? Let's Not Be Silly," Datamation, Vol. 12, No. 8, August 1966, pp. 124-125.

"A Special Report: New Uses for Computers in Business-Marketing, Finance, Administration, Scientific Decision Making, and Planning," Computer Decisions, Vol. 4, No. 1, January 1972, pp. 18-40.

rather than having the system designed to adapt to him. By now, the phenomenon of the Procrustean bed should be familiar to all. [7] The user finds himself continually modifying his requirements, sometimes for very necessary reasons, but frequently for the mere convenience of the EDP department. Only through user-EDP specialist teams, with all members being equal partners and each being respected for his special competence and contribution, can the full potential of new computer applications be realized.

It should not be assumed, however, that when a new system fails to live up to its potential, the fault lies solely with the EDP department. Quite the contrary; as with all business undertakings, the final responsibility lies with management. However, because of the pressures of day-to-day responsibilities, many managers will assign someone to the project team who is far from an ideal choice. Someone about to retire, a new hire, a displaced "excess" manager—all are examples of choices that will signal the organization that this new project has something less than management's total commitment. The results of such actions are not too difficult to predict. It is a common occurrence for managers to "have no time for that new project the EDP boys are dreaming up" only to find that they are forced to make time after the system is installed and it is having a serious impact on the operation of the business. Clearly, in such instances they have no right to claim "foul."

The following outline (a modification of remarks attributed originally to Harvey Golub of McKinsey and Company) is the all-too-true life cycle of a typical EDP application.

---

7. Procrustes was a giant in Greek mythology. When "offering a night's lodging to travellers, he would lay the short men on the large bed, and rack them out to fit it; put the tall men on the small bed, sawing off as much of their legs as projected beyond it. Some say, however, that he used only one bed, and lengthened or shortened his lodgers according to its measure." Robert Graves, The Greek Myths, Vol. 1, New York: George Braziller, 1959, pp. 329-330.

- Unwarranted enthusiasm

- Uncritical acceptance

- Growing concern

- Unmitigated disaster

- Search for the guilty

- Punishment of the innocent

- Promotion of the uninvolved

Summary

For management to be successful in the seventies, the focus must shift from efficiency to effectiveness; that is, doing the right thing rather than doing the thing right. Whereas efficiency is the conversion of inputs into outputs with as little loss as possible, effectiveness is the undertaking of activities which are congruent with the overall organizational goals and objectives.

Too often computer professionals are more interested in pursuing their own objectives than those of the organization. This results in projects being undertaken that may not address the most pressing problems of the enterprise. This misdirection of attention might well be labeled "committing a Type III Error," or solving the wrong problem.

In order to appraise the EDP health of an organization, it is necessary to measure both the costs and the benefits of the computer-related activities. This measurement, albeit not an easy task, is nevertheless an essential one—and yet many firms are relying on very crude data or are not making the attempt at all. In exploring possible benefits, systems designers should think in terms of making the most effective use of total corporate resources: material, equipment and facilities, capital, and people. And in the long run, the greatest gains should accrue to those systems which expand and enhance the decision-making ability of management.

GETTING THE RIGHT RESULTS FROM YOUR
DATA PROCESSING INVESTMENT--
THE CORPORATE VIEW

FRANK C. CARLIN

Director, Financial Operations
Lockheed California Company

INTRODUCTION

In preparation for this symposium I recently reviewed a similar presentation that I gave in Brussels to an organization called Management Centre/Europe, the European equivalent of the American Management Association. My earlier speech was in March 1965 and the subject then was "Communication Between The Manager and His Information System."

A review of background material used in this earlier talk clearly discloses that we have come a long way in the past seven years in terms of the relationship between top management and the data processing organization in a major corporation; however, we have not necessarily accomplished the goals that we set for ourselves in that time period, nor have we necessarily moved in exactly the same directions that were being predicted by the computer "experts" of 1965. Our progress, furthermore, has not been steadfast, but includes the retracing of many steps and some false starts and restarts along the way.

The interface today between top management and the computer is subject to considerably more realism and, for lack of a better word, compromise, than the kind of interface projected in the more "pioneer" days of the early 1960's.

Each party in the interface is now better able to work with the other. In many ways, we are approaching a semblance of maturity and stability, and we are in a better position to evaluate the quality of the computing job being done and to move ahead more effectively.

I will approach this discussion by postulating a somewhat idealized description or model of the role of top management in relation to the computer organization. After my model is developed, I will then present some observations as to why the model is not being achieved in its entirety and why both parties, the computing manager and the corporate executive, must be realistic in their expectations of what they are going to get from each other and how they can jointly take advantage of opportunities now ahead of them.

THE ROLE OF TOP MANAGEMENT

Top management, first of all, should set forth a set of fundamental goals for the corporation. These goals should be disseminated throughout the corporation. Top management should feel an obligation to contribute to the achievement of these goals in every way they can. Top management should be dedicated to successful interaction among the functions of the organization. They should know the unique contribution and value of each of these functions, one such function being the computing function.

Sometimes these contributions are readily measurable in quantifiable terms. When this is the case, top executives should insure that such numerical information is available to them in useful, summary form. They must be constantly concerned with quantitative success and failure, measurable strength and weakness, as related to various functions and components of the corporation. They should be alert to problem areas and to ensuring that appropriate solutions are found.

An effective corporate executive must also know how to deal with the nonquantifiable factors that permeate his organization. Examples of these are internal and external political considerations, employee morale, public image, and community service. These factors often impact on the computing manager as well.

With respect to the computing operation, top management must somehow be able to make judgments with respect to quantitative and nonquantitative success and failure. They must know the general nature of the flow of data into the EDP shop and, similarly, the flow of information back to its various users. It should be noted that top executives are usually not significant direct users of EDP data. Often their knowledge must be obtained second- or third-hand.

Top management must be able to discriminate among the levels of data processing decision making—for example, making very necessary and careful distinctions among problems relating to grand strategy, the highest level of managerial decision making and a level in which the top executive should be personally involved, and lower-level problems relating to specific systems, procedures, and even the detailed coding of instructions to the machine. The lower-level problems should not require his participation, yet he must somehow formulate judgments with respect to the managerial ability of his data processing staff—the ability to solve, among other things, the detail operating problems within the EDP function. Major failure can result from large-scale misjudgments at the detail level, creating catastrophe as great as errors in grand strategy.

A senior corporate executive should be constantly aware of the changes in his own economic environment, changes related to objectives and related to the tools with which he achieves those objectives. He must have adequate knowledge of the current technology that is available to the EDP operating manager; adequate knowledge should not necessarily mean detailed familiarity.

In regard to his overview of the computer, the senior executive must be ready to recognize and deal with many kinds of bias: bias, for example, that comes from fellow top managers, bias from "old guard" which is found in most large and established corporations, bias against change, bias against technology, bias against machines and systems and approaches that are unfamiliar and that sometimes appear threatening to the corporate establishment. He must also

deal with the counter-bias that can emanate from the data
processing organization, counter-bias that comes from being
out of the corporate mainstream, from a lack of perspective
of the company as a whole. Counter-bias results from looking too long inwardly with excessive emphasis on new and
exciting machines and tools and technology, from a perspective which underemphasizes service, profit, and accomplishing company goals.

Top management must participate in the breakdown of
bias from both directions and in the resulting solution of the
communication problem. One solution to the communication
problem is to get senior executives to talk more with the professional specialists within their organization, including the
managers of the data processing organization. There has
been a lot said about the difficulty that the EDP manager experiences in communicating with top management and what
steps he should take to improve that communication gap.
There has been too little said about what steps top management should take to assist in closing that gap.

Finally, top management must accept final responsibility
for success or failure of the various organizations within the
corporation, including the computing organization. They
must, therefore, participate in the grand strategy of that organization in the same manner that they participate in fundamental policy decisions affecting the traditional functional
organizations, such as marketing and finance. Accepting
such responsibility involves the use of follow-up to ensure
that organizational subgoals are achieved and that correc-
tive action plans are developed when the subgoals appear
threatened.

IMPERFECT LINE OF COMMUNICATION

That's the model and I'll be the first to admit that it
probably does not exist in perfect form in any major corporation. The shortfall, in fact, between the theoretical and
the real models is substantial. Many things have gone
wrong. There is a substantial variance between the potential of the interface—between top management and the data
processing manager—and the fulfillment of this interface.

Much of the problem relates to communication; however, each party over the years has probably expected too much from the other, particularly in the first decade of business computing, from 1955 to 1965.

The corporate executive today often has a very imperfect line of communication with the data processing organization. The negative information flows upwards in the organization more easily than the positive. The executive hears, usually second- or third-hand, about computer "foul-ups," incorrect data, and missing reports. He learns that information that he wants or needs is not available because the computer won't allow it.

The executive does not understand the evolutionary nature of the EDP implementation process. From the user's standpoint, it often takes years for a system to become successfully automated. Meanwhile, the user is often left to his own resources to make a system work. This difficult period of "crutched" semi-automation is the result of inexperience on the part of both user and systems planner with respect to each other's sphere of work.

The executive learns that total computer costs are exceeding what has been planned, and that there is no way to reduce these costs without almost catastrophic consequences. He is unable to get a meaningful analysis of what the computer operation is really costing the company, and the explanation he obtains with regard to cost overruns is unconvincing. Cost reduction and cost justification data are elusive. Computer costs seem only to be going up; they can never go down. Yet each generation of equipment is supposed to bring impressive savings in processing time and "quantum jump" increases in capability.

Usually, the positive contributions of the computer organization are not adequately publicized. From the corporate executive viewpoint, they do not come to the surface. They are lost in the noise level of routine lower-level operating reports. Furthermore, whereas the late 1950's and early 1960's witnessed some spectacular achievements in business data processing in the computerization of many routine clerical functions and in the achievement of substantial personnel savings, the more recent years have produced little that is spectacular from the vantage point of senior management.

Recent EDP history can be characterized by quiet success in the form of evolutionary gains: machine and software refinements, the application of improved documentation and internal standards, better scheduling, and equipment utilization. Unfortunately, these are not achievements that lend themselves to fanfare. They are often couched in technical jargon and provide an inadequate measure by which top management can determine success or failure. Furthermore, they have not necessarily resulted in better service to management or greater profits for the company. These refinements typically have had their greatest impact within the EDP function itself.

OPPORTUNITIES

I should now like to present some opportunities that currently exist for improving the corporate-computing interface. One such opportunity is the current trend of bringing the corporate manager and his staff into direct contact with the computer through the use of various on-line terminals. I believe these terminals are going to proliferate in the next 20 years in the same manner as home TV sets have spread in the last 20 years. These terminals provide opportunity for many organization levels to utilize the benefits of the computer without the constraints imposed by the data processing organization: the traditional chain of command, the paperwork bureaucracy, inflexible computer schedules, rerun problems, and the like.

The computer will become a very personal and personally convenient servant. In our own company we have recently made good progress in the use of these terminals by financial personnel—making cash flow studies, overhead projections, and special forecasts. Often the turnaround time using direct-access terminals, between the identification of the need for computer assistance and the resulting analysis, has been within the same working day. These terminals have done a lot to gain greater acceptance of the computer by the more traditional members of management at all levels.

I think we have a long way to go in utilizing the benefits of direct man-machine relationships throughout the corporation. We have given too much emphasis to machine optimization, for example, and to the processing of large quantities of data and voluminous reports. We have given too little emphasis to manager optimization; however, as the manager gains direct access to the computer, this neglect will be overcome. The manager, in effect, will be allowed to optimize himself, utilizing the computer.

Another opportunity that we have so far approached only on a very preliminary and superficial basis is the use of the computer for industrial and managerial training purposes. A contemporary English author, Norman Macrae, writing in the January 22, 1972, issue of the Economist magazine, estimates that our scientific and technical knowledge is increasing at a rate of 7% a year. If one accepts this premise, the conclusion can be reached that knowledge is doubling every 10 years and that the technically oriented executive at the peak of his career, between age 50 and 55, for example, cannot rely on the knowledge obtained in college and graduate school 30 years earlier since the knowledge that was in existence at that time is now only one-eighth of the contemporary knowledge with which he should have some familiarity. This type of obsolescence, at least in an advanced-technology industry, provides a real opportunity for bringing senior managers and the computer closer together.

The computer provides teaching capabilities and potential which are largely untapped in the corporate environment. The use of the computer for management, technical, and professional training at all levels should increase exponentially in this decade. This may contribute substantially to closing the gap between top management and the computer.

I also foresee that the major computer manufacturers will help us in improving the corporate-computer interface in that they are going to upgrade their marketing strategy from selling hardware and software to selling service. In the past their market strategy and product planning have often seemed to start with the internal memory of the computer as a focal point rather than with the needs of the commonplace, frustrated corporate manager. The emphasis has been on "What Can the Machine Do?" rather than "What Does the Manager Need?"

ORGANIZATIONAL REFORM

The greatest opportunity of the 1970's, from both points of view, may be in the area of organization. I don't think that top management in the typical corporation has done enough to organize itself in such a way as to assume its proper interface responsibilities vis-a-vis the computer oganization and, equally important, it has failed to organize itself effectively to receive benefits from the computer and its related support organization. There seems to be little thought given to adapting to new organization forms which permit effective use of new managerial technologies. It appears that traditional organizational forms are somehow considered sacred and inherently justifiable.

Our information technology is incompatible with the organization structure and communication patterns it attempts to serve. One by-product of information technology has been greater centralization of control, with top management gradually assuming many of the coordinative and control functions formerly performed by intermediate managerial levels. The new technology has gradually diminished the degree to which operating data is filtered and buffered by lower levels in traditional manual systems. If data is manipulated in today's systems, the probability is great that the manipulation occurs at the data source and that integrity occurs beyond the point of data capture.

From the standpoint of the data processing manager, great success has been attained in the mechanical collection, purification, and processing of data. The efficient dissemination or diffusion of this data throughout the corporation, however, is still at the pioneer state. The computing staff should critically examine this diffusion problem at the same time that the corporate organization reviews its traditional organizational forms and practices. I believe that data processing organizations are typically not organized in the manner which maximizes service to the user. Their organization structure also prevents maximum professional growth and personal effectiveness within the computing staff.

The corporate level should be more concerned with the organizational environment within the data processing shop. It is my opinion that data processing managers do not give enough attention to the organization, training, and motivation of their people, particularly of the people performing the more creative and unstructured functions within their organizations. Some of the greatest achievements that my company has experienced in the data processing area have been the result of innovative thinking by employees.

As our data processing organizations have grown, and our methods of operating have become more formal, I believe traditional organizational patterns have discouraged professional people from trying to reach out, from achieving their personal and company potential. In terms of organizational analysis, there seems to be a need for a better balance between the creative environment and operational efficiency. We have not yet found that balance in our company, and I suspect many firms find themselves similarly challenged.

Furthermore, the technical capabilities of a successful programmer or analyst are not necessarily the qualities required of a good manager. Often, computing personnel have been advanced into managerial roles for the wrong reasons.

In the introduction of this speech, when I was attempting to develop a top management model, I referred to "grand strategy," describing the highest level of decision making about computers and computer personnel. This is the level in which the data processing manager and the corporate executive jointly participate. I believe that the development of such a strategy has been greatly neglected. Is the data processing capability of a corporation a product line or strictly an internal tool? Can it be a source of revenue or must it be reviewed as a component of overhead expense? Often, the data processing organization within a corporation represents the annual expenditure of millions of dollars and the aggregation of unusual talents among several hundred professional employees. Are some of these talents unique? Do we have capability and technology within our data processing shop that we should market? Might the reverse also be true, that an external marketing strategy, if successful, might ultimately improve our internal capability?

COST SOPHISTICATION

The computing function within the large corporation no longer has the pioneer characteristics of ten years ago. Both the function and our attitude towards the function have matured. In view of this maturity, another area requiring more sophistication is computer cost analysis and cost justification.

I recently reviewed a very humorous article which summarized the false premises that have served as the economic justification of many computer installations and systems conversions in the past. I recommend to your amusement the article "The Savings Game" by Phil Philo (a pseudonym) in the February 1970 issue of Management Accounting. Here is a list of some of the ploys used by computer managers in obtaining corporate approval for various projects:

1. We were gonna (the employee ghosts)

2. Pick a number

3. Intangible benefits

4. Partial people

5. Jargon jitney

6. "Disappearing" jobs (to other organizations)

7. Pair up (soft savings with hard savings)

8. Savings are forever (no time limit)

9. Live it up (increased quantity or quality)

The gamesmanship that necessitates the use of such ploys is really the responsibility of corporate management. They have been negligent in not establishing clear, straightforward economic criteria by which computing proposals may be evaluated. These proposals should be viewed in the same manner as other investments of economic resources within the company. This has often not been the case in the past. Both parties to the corporate-computing interface have been kidding each other.

In our desire to obtain full benefit from our computer installations and to attain the same "state of the art" as our competition, many such computer investment decisions have been made more or less intuitively. Subsequently, the facts and justification logic have been produced to support the decision. This amateurish, "early pioneer" intuitive approach to computers has been prevalent at both the corporate and the operating levels in many corporations. We need to become more thorough and more scientific, practicing what we have been preaching to others; more important, we must approach this decision making with more honesty towards one another.

Top management has frequently been too easily convinced that expensive upgrading of equipment is necessary, providing the corporation with <u>more</u> capability for <u>more</u> dollars. There should have been greater insistence on <u>more</u> capability for <u>fewer</u> dollars. In some cases, the economic picture has probably called for less capability for <u>disproportionately fewer</u> dollars!

Corporate negligence has extended to cost tracking and control once the proposed application has been approved. I believe there is inadequate feedback of cost data relating to conversion and implementation phases of computer systems installations. Consequently, little effort is expended in postinstallation cost validation and in improving the accuracy of cost data in subsequent proposals. The naivete and, if you will allow me, simple-mindedness of our economic analyses are in sharp contrast to the sophistication we display with respect to economic ordering quantity, financial-return-on-investment decisions, and similar applications of the scientific method in other management areas.

UTILIZING THE AUDIT STAFF

Another opportunity available to top management is to make more effective use of the corporate internal auditing organization. This staff of professionals can provide substantial assistance in closing the corporate-computing communication gap. Most internal auditing organizations today have been developing a competence in the computing area. Often several auditors on a company staff have gained some specific experience in programming and EDP systems planning. They are familiar with the technical jargon of EDP specialists. Other auditors have gained computer exposure through outside educational programs. They have developed specialized skills in reviewing complex operations, applying appropriate criteria, and forming reasonable judgments about computer applications.

Internal auditors are also trained in the more general language of top management and in the art of written communication. The auditor can provide assistance in the substantiation of application proposals, in providing an independent appraisal, and in postconversion review and follow-up.

The role assigned to the auditor should be continuing and broad in scope. Audit techniques and related analysis and review can help to identify instances of misuse of EDP equipment, faulty systems design, and computer applications that do not provide the economic benefits originally intended. The watchword of the auditor's role should be <u>effectiveness</u>.

MANAGEMENT THEORY PENDULUM

The last few years, I believe, have witnessed much disillusionment with the utilization of the computer in improving clerical and other operational systems and with related quantitative approaches to management theory. In spite of the computer, in spite of the availability of many new decision-making techniques, in spite of voluminous data available to us almost at our fingertips, the corporate manager seems to continue making the same number of mistakes, and mistakes of the same magnitude. If anything, our job performance seems to have often deteriorated. Declining profit margins may be evidence of this.

We are too easily convinced that bad operating results are the outgrowth of economic conditions, foreign competition, and other exogenous factors, where, in many cases, we should be looking more critically at the way we perform our jobs. A greater appreciation of the magnitude of the impact of the quality of management is obtained from comparing income statements of similarly situated companies in the same industry, one considered "well managed" and one considered to have only "marginal" management.

The disillusionment with the systems and quantitative approaches is partly attributable to the overly optimistic and enthusiastic reception given to computers and quantitative techniques in their first decade, from 1955 to 1965. There was at that time a considerable amount of overselling, overcomputing, overspending, and perhaps overeducating.

More recently, with narrowing profit margins and unsettled economic conditions, the pendulum has probably swung back too far in the direction of short-run economies, and hard-boiled conservative attitudes. It is my hope that we are now entering a third period, a period of reasonable and balanced attitudes towards computer management and innovation where investments can be made that will have a substantial and tangible payoff, appreciated by all levels of the organization.

GETTING THE RIGHT RESULTS FROM YOUR

DATA PROCESSING INVESTMENT--

THE DP SHOP VIEW

LeROY RODGERS

Manager, Computer Programming
North American Rockwell

My topic, "The Data Processing Shop View," appears quite broad relative to our conference theme and even to the title of this session. Thus, my first task in preparing this presentation was to profitably narrow the scope of my remarks to be germane but not confine myself to simply organizing and summarizing things you already know. I hope to provide, not necessarily "THE data processing shop view," but at least "A data processing shop view," which is relevant to our session and contains perhaps one or two perspectives which are important but frequently overlooked.

Let me outline some of the tempting subjects I have decided not to talk about. First, I'm not going to talk about how to decide what is the right job to do. Essentially, that is the theme of this conference. I assume that you recognize that this task is larger than your data processing shop, that every organization needs to define somehow how it selects the order of data processing tasks to spend money and talent on. I assume that elsewhere in this conference you will hear more about how to improve this particular process. Second, I am not going to harangue you with another lecture on how to apply classical management principles and techniques to data processing problems—although that will be implicit in much of what I say. Third, I am not going to provide a summary recitation of mistakes made in the past and still being made today. We can exchange "war stories" elsewhere.

Instead, I do want to concentrate on the unique contributions that the data processing shop can make toward "Getting the Right Results From the Data Processing Investment" made by your organization.

I will start by assuming that some procedure encompassing more than the data processing shop has been used to decide the "right results" that are desired. That is, we in data processing will have had defined to us already what applications are to be added or altered, when they should be in place, what the performance expectations are, etc. —and we probably participated in that decision process, more or less. Our unique responsibility, then, is generally twofold:

1. Provide all the technical facilities needed to support the implementation and operation of the desired applications;

2. Minimize the total investment made to provide those facilities.

Of course, these responsibilities are not unique to data processing; they apply to any service unit in an organization. They are unique with respect to the special services and facilities we are concerned with.

Let's examine them more closely. In order to provide the technical facilities that are needed, data processing management must know the total computing requirements for the overall organization, projected sufficiently into the future for planning purposes. They must assure that this planning is coordinated across all potential users.

One approach to identify all the requirements is to work from the outside in—like peeling an onion. The outermost layer consists of those changes in facilities which are needed directly by the users. Generally, this includes such things as new and revised applications, data bases, and files—and occasionally new equipment, such as devices to capture input data or present output information.

The next layer under that consists of those resource

expenditures which are needed to implement the changes in facilities already identified. These generally include the most obvious cost elements—personnel to develop the new or revised programs, hardware sufficient to satisfy new workload requirements, and possibly the purchase of external services.

The next layer under that consists of the facilities and efforts necessary to support all those changes already defined. This need encompasses a number of not-so-obvious factors, neglect of which can add greatly to the true costs or cause delays in achieving the targeted installation. This category includes such elements as new or revised software, development of new procedures and forms, training of personnel, and timely and adequate coordination of all those concerned. The latter includes verbal and written communications, tentative plans and comments thereon, and meetings—all of which cost money and time.

After getting all these requirements identified across all applications, we must put them all together into a time-phased plan and schedule the activities needed to put them in place. This sounds relatively straightforward and shouldn't take us more than a week or two each year, assuming, of course, that no recycling or adjustments to the plan are necessary. For now, we will not concern outselves with the many problems that prevent us from satisfying all the identified "requirements"—facilities not available when scheduled, contention for critical resources, leveling of peak needs, and, of course, exceeding permitted budget levels. Naturally, at a conference like this we can assume anything we please, regardless of what really happens back home.

So much for the first responsibility I identified—providing all the technical facilities needed to support the implementation and operation of desired applications. Now let's examine our second general responsibility—to minimize the total investment made to provide those facilities.

There are a number of obvious costs associated with the installation and operation of computing facilities. In the case of hardware components, there are all the one-time costs associated with the initial installation into the complex; then there are the continuing rental or lease costs, operating costs, and maintenance costs. In the case of software components, similar costs can be reckoned and provided for, except that maintenance costs are often neglected. Similarly, when installing new or revised applications, one may plan and track the costs of development and implementation, the costs of production operation and, in some installations, the costs of continuing maintenance.

Another perspective we might try in looking at our responsibility to provide required facilities at minimum cost is to note what changes and what does not. If a facility is not changed, we have only half the problem; it is already there and our task is to minimize its cost. This ought to be relatively easy, and in many other fields it is. After all, we should be able to measure the performance of a given facility, compare it with some reasonable expectations, and identify means of eliminating or reducing the disparity. Unfortunately, we are only beginning to solve this "simple" problem—but there are hopeful signs of discipline and product technology emerging.

Mostly, however, we are concerned with the impact of change. Any change in our basic facilities costs—and the challenge is to find all those costs and control them. Costs, incidentally, may appear as either increased dollars or decreased capabilities.

Many changes are characterized as conversion efforts and, while some reaction is necessary to cope with any change, it isn't always recognized under the label "conversion." When we alter hardware or software facilities, we normally recognize conversion costs. We also recognize when we alter applications that we have conversion costs in both programs and files. We do not always recognize that forms and procedures and interfaces with people also may be changed, resulting in more indirect conversion costs. Similarly, we don't always recognize the impact of change in upper management, with possibly new policies and goals and procedures which are reflected in conversion efforts down through the organization.

Let's look more specifically at the area of responsibility unique to the DP shop—the impact of changes in computing facilities, either in increased cost or diminished capability.

There are a number of more hidden costs which, if visible, may easily have a greater impact than those already described. One factor many managers attempt to evaluate closely when investigating new facilities is their reliability. A committee in GUIDE, concerned with long-range requirements for computing facilities, studied this area about two years ago. Their report, distributed through both the GUIDE and SHARE Secretary's Distribution, took the approach that the larger concern to the user should be the availability of the system facilities he paid for and expected to use. While reliability is an important part of this concern, it is not enough.

Reliability may be viewed as designing and building components so as to minimize failures. One common measure of this factor in hardware is the classical "mean time between failures." In addition, however, there are a number of other factors associated with the fact of failure of a component. Can preventive maintenance be performed to avoid future failures? If a failure occurs, how easy is it to get the failure corrected? (A common measure is "mean time to repair.") Once repaired, what other efforts must be made to recover from the effects of a failure and get the system back to a point where the failure occurred? That is, what must be done to correct the secondary damages to both system facilities and your own application programs and data endangered by the component failure?

This report viewed all parts of the system provided by the supplier—hardware components, software components, documentation (which is the system to most users), and finally, an overall view of the total system complex. In addition to the factors associated with failure I have already described, it mentioned several other factors which might affect the apparent availability of your computing system facilities. These included: delivery of all needed components in time to establish the expected system complex; the time required to set up any particular facility for usage by an application; the ease of moving a particular component from one location to another and integrating it into a usable complex; and finally, the degradation to availability resulting from continual conversion requirements. Thus, this report addressed the need of the user to have available system facilities he can depend upon "to supply complete, correct results when required."*

Another subject this GUIDE committee is currently addressing, which has a hidden impact on costs in using facilities, is the usability of the facilities they install. As the technology continues to develop, we in using organizations find that we continue to extend the interface with computing facilities more and more throughout our organizations; more and more individuals and functions are relating directly to the usage of computing system facilities. "Facilities" here includes all components of the computing complex—both hardware and software. In procuring these facilities and using them, we can identify a number of the functions that must be performed; all of them cost money, and they can cost a good deal more in time and money if our people don't have what they need to do their job. If we propose to make any changes in these facilities, we should attempt to determine what the effects will be throughout our installation.

Someone must plan for the acquisition and installation of any new computing facility. To do this, he needs good information and he needs it in time to plan for all related problems. Someone must provide for its actual installation and preparation for usage after it arrives. If you are talking about a piece of hardware, this includes site preparation and facility planning with appropriate hardware engineers. If it is a piece of software, you are impacting your systems programmers, possibly your operations people, and very probably your applications programmers. Once the facility is installed, it has to be maintained. This may be something you hire out, as is normally done with hardware, or you may have to do a large part yourself. Also, some people must be concerned with the actual operation and usage of the facility. Others must be concerned with managing it as a new resource to be used effectively. Then there are

---

*User Strategy Evaluation Committee, "Requirements for Availability of Computing Facilities," GSD-22 (GUIDE Secretary's Distribution), November 1970.

the problems associated with training people who have contact with the new facility—both in the initial one-time installation aspect and in the continuing maintenance of skills and knowledge. And finally, there is the impact of the new facilities on those we might call application users, that is, those who interface directly with applications run on your complex and who may be affected by this new system facility.

Can we adopt any general concepts or policies to help minimize these costs of change? Indeed we can, provided we don't expect simple formulas or pat answers to apply to all situations.

One principle we should try to follow is to minimize the kinds of facilities we maintain in our inventory. Inevitably, in selecting tools and facilities one must consider trade-offs between the gains to be made with a large inventory of specialized facilities, and the necessary expenses of supporting them, versus a smaller number of more general-purpose facilities, which are easier and cheaper to maintain. A large airline does not necessarily add one copy of one model of airplane to its fleet simply because it is the most economical in operation over one given route. Similarly, we should not add one language or one device type or one operating system to our repertoire simply to optimize one particular usage—unless the gain outweighs the added costs and difficulties associated with its installation and continuing support requirements. The message in this point, then, is to generalize facility usage to the maximum feasible extent.

Another helpful concept is that of standardization. The places to create standards are between different kinds of facilities and between system facilities and people. To the extent you are successful in standardizing on these interfaces you may interchange components on either side of the interfaces.

A third principle in minimizing costs is simply to plan so as to minimize risk. If you plan to add new capabilities, you should assure that they are proven, that they will be available when you need them, and that they enjoy a wide acceptance with a high probability of continuity in the future. A corollary to this latter principle is that all planning for installation of new capabilities must include provision for alternate fail-safe courses of action.

In summary, perhaps if we in the DP shop can succeed in "doing our thing right," we will make an important contribution toward "doing the right thing" for our employer organizations.

EVALUATION OF HARDWARE, SOFTWARE, AND SOURCES OF SERVICE

PETER F. GUSTAFSON

Supervisor, Computer Software Planning and Control
Ford Motor Company

INTRODUCTION

The main theme of this symposium—"doing the right thing"—is addressed to what no doubt is of paramount concern in effective computer work. . . selecting the most useful applications. This too often has been downgraded in favor of more esoteric considerations in computer technology, resulting in efficient rather than effective computing. My topic, however, is not addressed to the theme of doing the right thing, but instead is concerned with doing the right thing right. In other words, this will be a discussion of the evaluation process as it relates to the selection and improvement of hardware and software resources. I am assuming that the right things to do have been previously determined, and thus will not consider this area further.

I am viewing the process of selecting and using computer resources from the standpoint of the corporate staff activity, in particular, the one at Ford Motor Company with which I am associated. In this capacity, we review proposals from computer activities throughout the company to acquire the computer tools to process their applications. These activities are highly varied, not only in terms of the types of applications, but also in the type of installation, ranging from small, single-computer shops to large, multimachine, service-bureau-like operations. In total, this reflects nearly three hundred computers representing virtually all major equipment manufacturers.

In reviewing these proposals, we attempt to make sure that the proper alternatives are considered, that the most effective alternative is selected, and that the selection process and results are in line with overall corporate objectives. Other staff activities are responsible for the appropriation of funds to implement the proposals which we have approved.

Before proceeding, I think it is important to define the key terms—evaluation, hardware, software, and services— to eliminate possible ambiguities and misinterpretations. Evaluation is the process of examining and judging the value of alternative approaches based on specified objectives and criteria. Evaluation is closely related to selection, in that, hopefully, the alternative which is selected is that which, based on the evaluation, most nearly satisfies the objectives and criteria.

The term hardware refers to electronic and electrome- chanical devices such as the CPU, memory, tape drives, disk drives, card readers, and printers. Software, in the general sense, means computer programs, be they operat- ing systems, languages, utilities, or user applications. In the sense that I will be using the term, software excludes the application programs. Looked at another way, it is the tools with which the applications are developed and imple- mented. These tools may be provided by the vendor supply- ing the equipment or by an independent vendor, or they may be developed in-house. Admittedly, there is a question in some areas whether a feature should be considered as hard- ware or software. Rather than getting into this, let it suf- fice that this will not be pertinent to the ensuing discussion.

The term services refers to people engaged in supporting all aspects of computing, including hardware, software, ad- ministration, systems, programming, operations, and main- tenance. This is the category into which the development and implementation of the applications fall. We thus have the three basic categories of computing—hardware, software, and services—which will be considered in terms of doing the right thing right.

GENERAL CONSIDERATIONS

The relative costs of the three resource categories are important to keep in mind during the evaluation process. The services category is typically the most expensive in today's environment, followed by hardware and software in that order. Examination of several surveys of computer users shows that the services category accounts for 55 to 60% of total data processing expenditures, hardware 30 to 40%, and other, only a small portion of which is for software, 5 to 10%. The importance of these cost relationships becomes evident when we consider the interrelationships and trade-offs among the three categories.

That there are interrelationships and trade-offs among hardware, software, and services is an accepted fact. Certain hardware features facilitate the development of software, and thus, lower its cost. Software, in turn, facilitates the development and implementation of the applications, which as I've defined it, is in the services category. All too often, however, these trade-offs are ignored and the evaluation addresses only the hardware category. This could be a costly mistake. Hardware, remember, represents only 30 to 40% of the total affected costs.

To carry this point further, the biggest trade-offs occur between the software and services categories. Using appropriate software tools can often result in an order of magnitude reduction in manpower effort for developing and implementing a given application. This is especially true when generalized application packages are available which can perform the tasks selected to be done on your system. Not all equipment vendors have the same availability or types of software products, either produced by them or by independent concerns.

EVALUATION PROCESS

After these introductory remarks, I'd like to move into the evaluation process itself. As I mentioned earlier, in an evaluation, the values of alternative approaches are examined and judged, based on specified objectives and criteria. This, in turn, is followed by the selection of the best alternative.

The first step in an evaluation is establishing the objectives and criteria for the evaluation. There are several hierarchies of objectives, with the highest level often being implied rather than explicitly stated. At this level, the objectives are the overall ones of the enterprise. Usually, they are stated as some form of "maximize profits." The maximization of profits can be achieved by reducing costs, avoiding future costs, increasing revenues with a proportionately lower increase in costs, or combinations of these.

Lest I be accused of overconcern for the maximization-of-profits philosophy, let me hastily add that profit does not necessarily imply dollars. What it does mean is dependent on the mission or goal of the corporation or institution. In some cases, this may take the form of enhancing social values or providing better services. The remaining levels of objectives are in line with the main objective and support it on a more detailed basis, such as implementing specific actions deemed to serve the main objective. It is important to determine the objectives and to keep them in perspective throughout the evaluation. Otherwise, it will be difficult, if not impossible, to make the best selection.

The criteria of the evaluation provide the guidelines and measures for satisfying the objectives. Thus, they must be stated in terms related to the objectives. Meaningful criteria are essential to constructing the specifications for developing the right alternatives to consider in the evaluation. The criteria, then, become the most important single ingredient in the evaluation process. Because of this, considerable attention will be devoted to this area.

In order to be effective, the objectives and criteria must be stated in terms of a common denominator, the most convenient and meaningful of which is dollars. At Ford Motor Company, we find that so doing greatly simplifies the task of comparing the various alternatives. Using dollars as the common denominator, with an objective of selecting the lowest-cost alternative which satisfies the goal of implementing the right things, would necessarily result in criteria stated in terms of the cost of the resources employed to achieve this objective.

The framework within which the evaluation takes place has a strong bearing on the factors to be considered. Basically, there are four environmental categories: Use of current resources; Upgrade of current resources; Replacement of current resources; and Addition of new resources. The evaluation process differs considerably, depending on the category. Use of current resources pretty much eliminates the possibility or need for an evaluation, although one may still be helpful in assessing the viability of the resources in terms of potential alternatives.

An upgrade of current resources offers somewhat more of an opportunity for evaluation, especially in terms of "plug-to-plug" compatible equipment and alternative financing arrangements. Replacement of current equipment is perhaps the most common category, and lends itself well to evaluation. Accordingly, this category will be given primary emphasis in the remainder of the discussion. Addition of new resources certainly demands a thorough examination. This category, however, is similar in many respects to the replacement of current resources, and, therefore, the forthcoming points of discussion will be equally well suited to it.

In order to make the most effective selection from among the various alternatives, all relevant costs must be identified and taken into consideration. This whole area will be given considerable attention later. Likewise, appropriate evaluation tools should be applied in order to quantify the computing environment and take a lot of the "guesswork" out of specification development.

We now come to what I consider the key to the whole evaluation process—the concept of functional requirements. A functional requirement is a specific goal, function, or task which the computing system is to accomplish for the users of the system. Taken collectively, they are those things which the applications are to accomplish. That is, providing effective information processing service where and when needed—doing the right thing. Functional requirements relate to the applications rather than to the capabilities of the resources. They form both the application objectives and the evaluation criteria. They are used as the basis for developing the specifications upon which to develop the alternatives.

Considering the importance of a common denominator for the evaluation process (in our case dollars), the costs of the functional requirements become the ingredients which form the evaluation criteria. As such, these criteria automatically take into account the trade-offs among the hardware, software, and services categories. To clarify what I mean by this, consider the following example. Assume one of the functional requirements of an application is to communicate interactively with terminal users. Allowing for certain basic hardware characteristics, the bulk of this facility would be provided by computer programs. It could be integrated into the operating system, provided by an independent software product, custom-developed, or a combination of all three. It is immaterial how this facility is implemented, as long as the combination which yields the lowest cost of providing that functional requirement is selected. This contrasts with specifying criteria, such as the operating system must have time-sharing capabilities, or a high-level interactive language must be available, or the hardware must have virtual memory capabilities. I don't want to imply that these aren't important, but their values would better be assessed and measured in terms of the cost of the corresponding functional requirement.

The cost of a functional requirement is the sum of the individual costs of the resources required to implement that function. Minimizing this cost necessarily reflects the optimum balance among hardware, software, and people for that requirement. In the above example, if the interactive terminal facility had to be implemented through the services category rather than by the operating system or a software product, the cost might be so much greater as to completely overshadow any hardware or other software advantages. The sum of the costs of all the functional requirements reflects the true value of an alternative. Selecting the alternative with the lowest of these costs would result in optimum use of hardware, software, and people.

In an evaluation with the objective of replacing existing equipment with a lower-cost alternative (if one exists), the following would be representative statements of functional requirements:

1. Process the following programs according to the indicated schedule, with maximum elapsed running times as stated. (A list of the application programs with run-time characteristics would be included here).

2. Support an on-line data base of X million characters.

3. Communicate with the following terminal devices. (A list of the actual devices and their characteristics would be included here).

4. Interface with the abc COM peripheral in a manner supporting all existing requirements.

5. For on-line application X, process an average of Y messages per hour with a peak of Z messages per hour.

6. For application X, provide average response time of Y seconds Z% of the time.

7. Allow full system recovery within X minutes in the event of one or more of the following errors or failures. (A list of these would be included here.)

8. Provide for a 20% growth in application Y message volume during the next year, with 10% per year thereafter, maintaining the same performance characteristics as are currently being obtained.

9. Provide printing capabilities of 1,200,000 print lines (full 132-character lines) per day, with peak processing capacity of 96,000 lines per hour for a sustained three- to four-hour period each day.

The above functional requirements are only a small sample of the types (many of which would be more specific and in more detail) which would be included in the evaluation. The important point to notice is that these requirements relate to the needs of the applications. They do not arbitrarily dictate what types of hardware, software, and services are required. The method by which a functional requirement is implemented by each alternative could be unique. The important point is the cost of providing that facility.

Let's take a closer look at some of the above sample statements of functional requirements in order to gain a better understanding of what they are and how they lead to a more effective selection. The requirement "Process the following programs according to the indicated schedule, with maximum elapsed running times as stated" is designed to accomplish the following:

1. Characterize each current program according to processing requirements, both for main-frame and peripheral devices.

2. Insure that each program can be run on the alternative system.

3. Stipulate a schedule, or time frame, within which each program must be run.

The requirement in no way dictates specific equipment configurations or operating system characteristics. It allows the alternate vendors to construct the system in what they consider the most effective manner, thus yielding the lowest-cost approach. If the CPU and peripheral devices were fast enough, it might be possible to satisfy this requirement by processing jobs in a serial rather than a multiprogramming mode (the cost would dictate the best approach). At least this option exists. Had a requirement of a multiprogrammed operating system been specified, this option would have been unnecessarily precluded (perhaps with a resultant cost penalty).

In the same vein, this requirement doesn't suggest CPU and memory characteristics. A fixed-word or variable-length CPU could be used. The instruction set could consist of twenty basic instructions or three hundred very sophisticated ones. Memory could be hierarchical or monolithic, with size less than, equal to, or greater than the largest programs. Segmentation, virtual memory paging, or other techniques could be employed to accommodate the existing programs. Again, the costs would dictate the best approach. The important point is that all current programs would be processed in the required time frames and at the lowest cost. To go beyond this opens the possibility for significant cost penalties and a less-than-optimum configuration.

The statement "Support an on-line data base of X million characters" (with added detail, of course, to completely specify the requirements) provides all the information necessary to develop a specific configuration, but does not imply what the actual device characteristics should be. Magnetic drums, fixed-head disk, movable-arm disk, removable or nonremovable disk packs, data cells, or any other suitable random-access device might be potential candidates. Again, the cost of performing this function would determine the best device or combination of devices to use.

The requirement "Communicate with the following terminal devices" would specify what devices must be supported, including number of simultaneous users, line speeds, transmission modes, and application program interface needs. It doesn't specify how this facility is to be implemented. It could be handled entirely by the hardware, could be provided through vendor-supplied software (either built into the operating system or superimposed as a separate package), provided by an independent vendor software product, custom-developed by the user, or combinations of these.

The hardware aspects of this could take many forms. It could be handled by a front-end processor or built into the CPU. Again, many options exist and none should be overlooked. That combination of hardware and software features yielding the lowest cost would be the most effective choice. When I say lowest cost, I mean total lowest cost. Included in these costs should be, for example, a computed amount for programmer effort to interface the application programs with whatever facility is proposed. A difficult interface might cause the cost of this effort to become very high. On the other hand, a simple interface could result in significantly lower costs to the point where it might more than offset somewhat higher hardware and software costs. All relevant costs of providing a function must be considered in order to determine the true costs of a functional requirement.

Looking at one more example—"Provide printing capabilities of 1,200,000 print lines (full 132-character lines) per day, with peak processing capacity of 96,000 lines per hour for a sustained three- to four-hour period each day"— we again see that specific equipment capabilities are not implied. This requirement could conceivably be satisfied by one 2200-line-per-minute printer, two 1200-line-per-minute printers, three six-hundred or six three-hundred-line-per-minute printers, by impact or nonimpact printing, and by on-line or off-line (or a combination of these) facilities.

In all of these examples, the important point is to satisfy the specific requirement in the most effective manner, that is, at the lowest cost, all factors being considered. I hope you can see from these examples how the functional-requirements approach achieves this objective.

Carrying the functional-requirements approach to the conceptual level implies freedom from all existing constraints and prior decisions. As a practical matter, however, there are some elements which need to be arbitrarily stated as requirements, even though in the abstract sense they need not be. An example of this might be in the area of programming languages. If an installation has standardized on a programming language, say COBOL, it might be impractical (although theoretically correct) to consider rewriting all programs in another language. In this type of case, then, one of the functional requirements might be stated as the need for a COBOL compiler.

In the abstract sense, the costs of going to a new language would be considered and offset by the advantages of the alternative requiring such a conversion. When formulating these arbitrary (but deemed necessary) functional requirements, extreme care must be taken to make sure they are definitely justified and are not unnecessarily precluding otherwise viable alternatives. Too many arbitrary functional requirements (in this sense arbitrary tends to imply specific hardware and software requirements rather than user requirements, which is the real intent of the term functional requirement) will result in approaching today's level of evaluation—namely, in terms of specific hardware and software facilities.

RELEVANT COSTS

All relevant costs of each alternative must be identified and taken into consideration. The cost of the functional requirements takes into account most of the essential costs, but usually there are some additional ones. Failure to recognize all costs can result in an improper selection. As I see it, there are six general categories of cost associated with the evaluation process, all of which must be considered. These are:

1. Evaluation costs

2. Installation costs

3. Conversion costs

4. Application development costs

5. Ongoing operating costs

6. Usability costs

The evaluation costs include all those associated with performing the evaluation. This would include developing the objectives and criteria, formulating the specifications, quantifying the environment, reviewing the results of the evaluation, and making the selection. Most of these costs are for internal manpower, although there could be out-of-pocket costs for consulting services as well. In any case, the evaluation costs should not be overlooked in terms of the total effort, and should be considered in relation to anticipated benefits, as it could well prove that the cost of an evaluation could exceed the potential benefits of the evaluation (in which case, of course, the evaluation should not be undertaken).

The installation costs are those associated with acquiring and implementing the selected alternative. By nature, they are one-time costs, and usually occur over a fairly short period of time. Included in this category would be site preparation, acquisition of any required software, and other miscellaneous related expenses, such as transportation charges and sales tax.

The conversion costs are all expenses incurred solely for the purpose of getting from the current environment to the new one. These costs, also, are by nature one-time costs, although they could (and usually do) spread out over a longer period of time. Included in this category would be the costs of any reprogramming, running duplicate facilities during the launch and check-out period, converting programs from one vendor's compiler to the other, changes in procedures, and training of personnel in the new equipment.

In most facilities replacement proposals that I've seen lately, conversion costs represent a large portion of the total financial picture and very often preclude going to lower-cost (on an on-going basis) alternatives from an overall economic standpoint. Too often conversion costs are underestimated or partially ignored (What about employe morale? Postponing of new applications? Unresponsiveness to changes in the business environment? Delayed and sometimes inaccurate output? Overtime expenses? —these all have real costs associated with them). Because of this, I can't emphasize too strongly the care that should be taken in properly identifying and quantifying the conversion costs.

The application development costs would be those incurred to launch new applications as specified by the evaluation criteria. Normally, the costs of the corresponding functional requirements would account for the hardware and software components of the new applications, but the people cost assessment would rest mainly with the user, based on the hardware and software facilities provided. This, too, is a key area because of the trade-offs available in terms of software and services. Here is where the user should be diligent in specifying appropriate functional requirements for facilitating application development and in assessing accurately the costs of working with the resultant tools.

Ongoing operating costs encompass those related to running the applications. Included, of course, would be equipment rental (don't forget extra-use charges, property taxes, maintenance costs, etc.) and expenses for operations personnel. Also included in this category would be the systems and programming costs for maintaining the existing applications and software systems.

I have included usability cost as a category because, since it is somewhat intangible by nature, it is often overlooked.

By usability cost, I mean what does it actually cost, in terms of people requirements, to use the various facilities provided by the environment? Is time wasted because of too many required redundant specifications? Is the interface to the computer simple and understandable, or is it overly complex and unwieldy? These types of intangibles should be assigned a value and the implied cost computed.

EVALUATION TOOLS

I mentioned earlier the importance of quantifying the computing environment, both current and planned, prior to undertaking an evaluation. There are several tools and techniques which facilitate this process and provide information which makes the evaluation more meaningful. Representative of these tools are simulation, hardware monitoring, software monitoring, and the more conventional approaches, such as running benchmark programs. In addition to providing input to the evaluation, certain of these tools are designed for optimizing the current environment as well. Doing so quite often eliminates the need for expanding existing facilities or adding new ones, thus obviating the need for the evaluation.

That proper quantification of the environment can eliminate much of the "guesswork" in developing specifications can be made evident by a recent example at Ford Motor Company. In this instance, a large, on-line data collection and dissemination system was being examined in terms of a large expected increase in message volume. At first, it was assumed that this system consumed a large portion of the CPU power on the current machine (an IBM 360/65), and thus would require a substantially larger machine (in this case an IBM 370/165) to handle the expected increase in message traffic. Applying our simulation and hardware monitoring tools to this system showed that, contrary to what everyone thought, this system consumed very little of the current machine, and even considering the increased message volume, would still put little demands on the CPU. The results of this analysis convincingly indicated that a 370/155 could easily handle the system instead of the more costly 370/165. In fact, a 370/145 could handle the job, except for the core requirements of this system.

Computer simulation is the most sophisticated approach to quantifying the environment. It is the only tool which effectively allows planned systems to be described and quantified as well as existing ones. It permits ready evaluation of alternative configurations and modes of operation. Use of this tool does, however, require a relatively large investment of effort. The most important aspect of the simulation approach is that systems and programs are defined in terms similar to functional requirements rather than related to specific hardware and software facilities.

Hardware and software monitoring serve to quantify the current environment only. Elements such as CPU utilization, channel utilization, peripheral utlization, and overlap of channels and CPU can readily be measured with relatively little effort. More extensive information can be obtained, of course, with more effort. Although both approaches provide similar types of information, there are some important differences. Hardware monitors are external to the equipment and thus do not degrade system performance while monitoring. They are limited, however, to measuring events based on availability of appropriate signal points. On the other hand, software monitors can tap into the operating system and obtain valuable information on system processing. Software monitors operate on a sampling basis as opposed to an actual count or timing basis as in the case of a hardware monitor. Both types of monitors are applicable, as each can do functions not available to the other.

Use of benchmarks can, at best, provide some indication of the ability of a proposed configuration to run existing programs and with what relative performance compared to current equipment. At worst, benchmarks can be very misleading. Extreme care should be taken in constructing a benchmark. The programs selected should be truly representative of the environment (a very difficult task). The equipment on which the benchmark is run should be identical to the proposed equipment. Devices with different speeds, different channel configurations, more or less memory, a different operating system, or other differences can completely invalidate the benchmark results. In no case should a benchmark be a substitute for the other quantification tools described above.

SOURCES OF SERVICE

Throughout the discussion, I have intimated that the functional-requirements approach takes into consideration the services category and optimizes that cost as well as the hardware and software costs by recognizing the trade-offs among the three categories. I don't want to imply by this that the user need not be aware of the available alternatives in the service category, because he, in fact, is the one who usually will be making the decisions as to what approach to take in conjunction with the proposed hardware and software facilities. What the functional requirements approach does do is identify what functions should be performed by each of the categories.

As I have defined service, it encompasses people engaged in supporting all aspects of computing, including hardware, software, administration, systems, programming, operations, and maintenance. All of these categories have alternate sources, each with varying costs. Of primary importance is the cost of obtaining these services. Secondarily, pragmatic issues, such as the ability to attract and retain qualified people, may dictate what alternatives are available.

There are four basic alternatives to providing services with company resources. These are (loosely categorized) equipment vendors, software vendors, consulting firms, and specialty firms. The types of services offered range from a specific area, such as supplemental programming services, to encompassing all areas, as in a complete facilities management approach. Several of these alternatives can be used concurrently. Again, cost is the prime factor to consider.

Equipment vendors often perform services other than just providing the machinery. In some cases, this is provided at no charge, or is substantially less than other alternatives (including in-house). Usually, services provided by the vendor are in the hardware, software, programming, and maintenance areas. Of special importance in an evaluation is what services the vendor will provide in converting to the new environment. This can have a substantial cost impact, plus or minus.

Software vendors and consulting firms vary in the areas served, but usually can best be utilized in those in which they have specific expertise, or for a short-duration increase of manpower. Don't overlook the possibility of having a software vendor modify one of his products to fit your environment and needs. This can often cost substantially less than doing it yourself.

The specialty firms address one or more specific areas, for example, hardware maintenance. Often, the services they provide are in competition with sources other than company resources. Here, again, the cost of providing the service is the essential factor to consider. The cost, of course, must include allowances for reliability, service responsiveness, and ability.

SUMMARY

In summarizing, I'd like to stress the concept of the functional-requirements approach as it relates to the evaluation of hardware, software, and sources of service. In so doing, I will go back over the more salient points relating to this, with hopes that this concept becomes clear and understandable.

In an evaluation, alternatives must be identified and objectives and criteria established for judging the relative value of each alternative. The objectives and criteria should be stated in terms of a common denominator, the most convenient and meaningful of which is dollars. If it is done, then an objective of selecting the lowest-cost alternative can be expected to result in criteria stated in terms of the cost of the resources employed to achieve this objective.

Selecting an alternative requires an analysis of the cost interrelationships, or trade-offs, among the hardware, software, and services categories. The key ingredient in all cases is the functional requirements of the applications, whether they be implemented by hardware, by software, or through services. Using the cost of functional requirements as the criterion automatically takes into account the trade-offs among the three categories. It is in terms of the cost of these functional requirements, then, that the evaluation criteria must be specified in order to select the most effective alternative.

The cost of a functional requirement is the sum of the costs of the resources required to implement that function. Minimizing this cost necessarily reflects the optimum balance among the hardware, software, and services categories for that requirement. The sum of the costs of all functional requirements reflects the true value of an alternative. Selecting the one with the lowest of these costs results in optimum use of computing resources.

To repeat, functional requirements are those things which the applications are to accomplish. That is, providing effective information processing where and when needed—doing the right thing. Functional requirements relate to the applications rather than to the capabilities of the resources. They form both the application objectives and the evaluation criteria. They are used as the basis for developing the specifications upon which to develop the alternatives. Only by providing this direct relationship can the most effective selection be made.

There are many aspects of the evaluation process, especially one as complex as selecting a computing environment. Using the cost-of-functional-requirements approach does not necessarily make the process easier, and in fact, may be more demanding. It does, however, lead to a better selection and provides a consistency of measure unattainable by other commonly used approaches. In my opinion, it is the only practical means for satisfying the goal of doing the right thing right.

EVALUATION OF THE EFFECTIVE
DATA PROCESSING SHOP

ROBERT S. FARMER

Director of Data Services
County of Orange
Santa Ana, California

INTRODUCTION

Thus far in this symposium, you have been challenged with the perplexing question: Are you doing the right thing? This challenge represents a significant threat not only to you but even more so to the users of the computing facility services. We, as data processing professionals, should be continually asking our customers this question. It is the ultimate responsibility of our customers to determine if we are "doing the right thing" for them.

I want to provide a slight change of pace and challenge you with the other half of the symposium title. How do you know you are doing your thing right? I believe the proper response to be through evaluation.

"Evaluation of the Effective Data Processing Shop" implies the comparison of current status with established goals and objectives. In order for staff and management to mutually set goals and objectives and thus have a yardstick to measure or evaluate against, method standards must exist for both the system development and operational activities of a data processing shop.

When asked to speak to this difficult question, I took one step back and asked myself, "What is the one major management factor I have observed over the years in what are

64

considered to be the effective data processing shops?" Although I have observed many approaches to management of a data processing shop, there is one factor that is outstanding among this respected class of effective shops. That is the existence of a set of comprehensive standards and procedures covering the entire systems development process.

NEED FOR STANDARDS AND PROCEDURES

We happen to deal in an environment that requires complex communication across many interfaces. Complex and detailed communications must occur throughout the entire systems development process:

USER REQUIREMENT—SYSTEM DESIGN—PROGRAM-

MING--SYSTEM TEST—IMPLEMENTATION—OPERA-

TIONAL—MANAGEMENT

If methods standards are not developed so that each member of the development team knows his functions and responsibility, I guarantee a failure will occur somewhere along the development path. The failure will vary in intensity from costly to disastrous.

ONE WORK-BREAKDOWN LIST

There are various management approaches to dealing with this problem. I would like to share one that we have tried that appears to be quite successful. The County of Orange is not unlike a large conglomerate. There are approximately 9000 employees in some 44 departments and special districts. Computer services are provided by a centralized data processing shop providing systems and programming operations to 32 departments. Each major user has at least one liaison analyst to communicate requirements and continued evaluation to the data processing department. One department, the Auditor-Controller, is the chief financial officer and therefore must be involved in the specifications for controls and audits of financial systems.

In order to deal effectively with the communications

problems involved in a complex organization concerning a technically complex subject, a two-part Systems Development Manual was developed to promote complete and concise information across each interface. Part I of the manual deals solely with the internal data processing procedure and is not distributed beyond the data processing department. Part II deals with the data processing department/user interface and is an organization-wide manual. There are 725 pages and 202 individual procedures in these two manuals.

Our initial efforts were directed at defining all the steps that should occur in most systems development projects. Top data processing management personnel were assigned this task. Then various data processing staff personnel were used to write the procedures necessary to define each step. Finally, the approach was coordinated with all our major users.

Earlier I said the systems development process was a complex interaction between the user and data processing and within the data processing organization. We first divided the systems development process into phases, then the phases into milestones, and finally the milestones into detailed tasks. The final outcome turned out to be:

	Phase	Milestones	Tasks
I.	System Proposal	5	37
II.	Management Review and Authorization	2	6
III.	System Design	6	41
IV.	System Test	4	30
V.	System Implementation	5	35
VI.	Operational	3	13
VII.	Post-implementation Review	3	3
		28	165

The following is a complete work-breakdown list used at the County of Orange for those who wish to explore the use of the Phase, Milestone, and Task approach.

SYSTEM DEVELOPMENT OVERVIEW:
Phases to Milestones

LEGEND

Responsibility	Type
UD = User Department	P = Phase
AC = Auditor-Controller	M = Milestone
DS = Data Services	T = Task

Function	Type	Responsibility
I. System Proposal	P	
Prepare request	M	UD
Review request and schedule analysis start date	M	DS
Define system requirements and benefits	M	DS
Define audit and control requirements	M	AC
Schedule systems development	M	DS
II. Management Review and Authorization	P	
Define proposed review schedule	M	DS
Submit system proposal and obtain authorization	M	DS
III. System Design	P	
Publish plan of action	M	DS
Define system at program level	M	DS
Identify data requirements	M	DS
Define detailed schedules	M	DS

Function	Type	Responsibility
Prepare procedures	M	UD/DS/AC
Program the procedures	M	DS
IV. System Test	P	
Supply input data	M	UD
Simulate production run	M	DS
Evaluate system test	M	UD
Approve system test	M	UD
V. System Implementation	P	
Convert data base	M	DS
Provide for organizational impact	M	UD/DS
Train personnel	M	DS/UD
Arrange for parallel operation	M	UD
Review and approve operational systems	M	UD
Implement operational system	M	UD
VI. Operational	P	
Set up a system schedule	M	DS
Plan for system changes	M	UD
Insert system audits	M	AC
VII. Post-implementation Review	P	
Compare actual vs. proposed benefits and costs	M	UD
Evaluate system effectiveness	M	UD
Make recommendations	M	UD

SYSTEM DEVELOPMENT DETAIL VIEW:
Milestones to Tasks

Function	Type	Responsibility
I. System Proposal	P	
Prepare request	M	
Review the decision to make request	T	UD
Identify problem area	T	UD
Define problems and acceptable performance standards	T	UD
Document existing work flow and identify paperwork	T	UD
Identify cost associated with documented work flow	T	UD
Identify design constraints	T	UD
Identify all reports to be included in proposed system	T	UD
Identify input data	T	UD
Determine frequency requirements	T	UD
Determine input data volumes	T	UD
Prepare TOP chart	T	UD
Define maximum cost of new system	T	UD
Determine need date	T	UD
Determine priority	T	UD
Define benefits of new system	T	UD
Complete request	T	UD
Review request and schedule analysis start date	M	
Assign analyst to review user department request	T	DS
Initiate system binder	T	DS
Estimate cost and schedule start date of analysis	T	DS
Review and approve	T	DS

Function	Type	Responsibility
Define systems requirements and benefits	M	
Review problem and verify specifications	T	DS
Complete definitions of output data	T	DS
Complete definitions of input data	T	DS
Verify frequency requirements	T	DS
Verify volume requirements	T	DS
Prepare SAP charts	T	DS
Review alternatives and verify approach	T	DS
Define audit and control requirements	M	
Verify system design constraints	T	DS
Define audit control requirements	T	AC
Define desired performance indicators	T	UD
Schedule systems development	M	
Develop a systems test plan	T	DS
Develop a plan for conversion and parallel operation	T	DS
Identify machine requirements	T	DS
Identify manpower requirements	T	DS
Develop a master schedule	T	DS
Identify cost of new system	T	DS
Identify benefits/costs of new system	T	DS

Function	Type	Responsibility
II. Management Review and Authorization	P	
Define proposed review schedule	M	
Determine review date	T	DS
Review proposal package	T	DS
Distribute proposal package	T	DS
Prepare presentation material	T	DS
Submit system proposal and obtain authorization	M	
Make presentation	T	DS
Obtain authorization	T	DS
III. System Design	P	
Publish plan of action	M	
Issue plan of action	T	DS
Define system at program level	M	
Finalize SAP charts	T	DS
Update WLC file	T	DS
Identify tape, disk, forms, and machine requirements	T	DS
Determine program priorities	T	DS
Initiate program binders	T	DS
Develop program definition	T	DS
Order tapes, disks, forms, and hardware	T	DS
Identify data requirements	M	
Identify report data elements	T	DS
Identify source document data elements	T	DS
Design report layouts	T	DS
Approve report layouts	T	UD
Prepare record layouts	T	DS

Function	Type	Responsibility
Define file organization	T	DS
Define source documents	T	DS
Identify source data edit requirements	T	DS
Define detailed schedules	M	
Develop detailed test plan	T	DS
Develop detailed implementation plan	T	DS
Develop training plan	T	U D
Develop organization plan	T	U D
Prepare procedures	M	
Develop keypunch procedures	T	DS
Develop production control procedures	T	DS
Develop source document control procedures	T	U D
Develop report utilization	T	U D
Develop audit control procedures	T	A C
Complete systems binder	T	DS
Review and approve systems binder	T	DS
Complete operations binder	T	DS
Review and approve operations binder	T	DS
Programming	M	
Review program binder	T	DS
Prepare logic charts	T	DS
Prepare debug-test data	T	DS
Approve logic charts	T	DS
Code program and desk-check coding sheets	T	DS
Keypunch coding sheets	T	DS
Compile and desk-check program	T	DS

Function	Type	Responsibility
Debug-test the program	T	DS
String-test program and segment	T	DS
Approve test results	T	UD
Complete program binder	T	DS
Review and approve program binder	T	DS
IV. System Test	P	
Supply input data	M	
Prepare input documents	T	UD
Control source documents	T	UD
Transport data	T	UD
Schedule job	T	
Simulate production run	M	
Receive, log, and control input data	T	DS
Keypunch/verify input data	T	UD/DS
Verify computer schedule	T	DS
Receive and control key-punched cards and documents	T	DS
Prepare job set-ups	T	DS
Pre-stage job stream	T	DS
Perform computer processing	T	DS
Perform forms handling	T	DS
Audit output products	T	DS
Distribute output products	T	DS
Store/dispose of input data	T	DS
Train personnel	M	
Re-evaluate training plan	T	UD/DS/AC
Prepare/finalize course outline & schedule	T	UD/DS/AC
Identify participating personnel	T	UD/DS/AC

Function	Type	Responsibility
Obtain training material and facilities	T	UD/DS/AC
Conduct training	T	UD/DS/AC
Evaluate system test	M	
Receive output reports	T	UD
Evaluate output reports	T	UD
Distribute output reports	T	UD
Determine accuracy of user procedures	T	UD
Evaluate forms effectiveness	T	UD
Evaluate Data Services operating procedures	T	DS
Evaluate training effectiveness	T	UD/DS
Upgrade programs, procedures, forms, & training	T	UD/DS/AC
Approve system test	M	
Approve output reports	T	UD
Approve system test	T	UD
V. System Implementation	P	
Convert data base	M	
Identify data-base files	T	DS
Identify conversion methods	T	DS
Develop conversion programs	T	DS
Identify manpower requirements	T	DS
Define machine requirements	T	DS
Convert mechanized data files	T	DS
Convert manual records	T	UD
Determine retention criteria for data base	T	UD
Evaluate accuracy of converted data files	T	UD

Function	Type	Responsibility
Provide for organizational impact	M	
Identify job skill requirements	T	UD/DS
Identify data volumes	T	UD/DS
Determine level of support	T	UD/DS
Determine work flow	T	UD/DS
Determine operating costs	T	UD/DS
Identify facility requirements	T	UD/DS
Provide for organization changes	T	UD/DS
Provide for personnel staffing	T	UD/DS
Train personnel	M	
Re-evaluate training plan	T	UD/DS/AC
Prepare/finalize course outline & schedule	T	UD/DS/AC
Identify participating personnel	T	UD/DS/AC
Obtain training material and facilities	T	UD/DS/AC
Conduct training	T	UD/DS/AC
Evaluate training effectiveness	T	UD/DS/AC
Provide for follow-on training	T	UD/DS/AC
Arrange parallel operation	M	
Identify parallel requirements	T	UD
Determine dual system methods	T	UD
Determine manpower requirements	T	UD
Identify machine requirements	T	DS
Process new system	T	UD
Process old system	T	UD
Determine file retentions	T	UD

Function	Type	Responsibility
Review and approve operational system	M	
Compare results of old and new systems	T	U D
Approve operational system	T	U D
Discontinue old system	T	U D
Implement operational system	M	
Allow for operational turn-over	T	U D
VI. Operational	P	
System scheduling	M	
Determine production status	T	DS
Make production forecast	T	U D
Adjust forecast	T	U D
Adjust production schedule	T	U D
Produce computer schedule	T	DS
Acknowledge adjustment	T	DS
System changes	M	
Produce work request	T	U D
Verify request	T	DS
Review request	T	U D/DS
Design change approval	T	DS
Modify program	T	U D/DS
Check for user acceptance	T	U D
System audits	M	
Compile audit analysis	T	AC
VII. Post-implementation review	P	
Compare actual vs. proposed benefits and costs	M	
Coordinate objectives	T	DS

Function	Type	Responsibility
Evaluate system effectiveness	M	
Evaluate system	T	UD/DS/AC
Review evaluation	T	UD/DS/AC
Make recommendations	M	

REACTION TO A STRUCTURED APPROACH

The reaction of most system designers will vary from mild acceptance to violent resistance when first confronted with a structured approach to systems development. After they objectively review the task, however, they come to the conclusion that most of the tasks really are accomplished during the course of most system development efforts. The question one must answer is "What is beneficial to the project: pre-plan and schedule the tasks appropriate for the project, or let the necessary tasks occur as someone on the team thinks they become necessary?" The answer, I think, is obvious.

The use of such an approach to systems development is strictly a methods standard, not a quality standard. Good system design will depend on the quality the designer exercises in accomplishing each task.

HOW DOES THE STRUCTURED APPROACH
FIT THE ORGANIZATION?

As one reviews the responsibilities we have assigned to each task, he will conclude that responsibility for each task would vary from one organization to another; however, we follow some general rules and responsibilities which would be appropriate for each project organization.

THE STEERING COMMITTEE

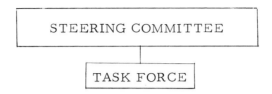

RULES FOR STEERING COMMITTEE

1. Composed of department heads only

2. Personnel must meet at least monthly

3. Chairman is from most impact user department

RESPONSIBILITIES OF STEERING COMMITTEE

1. Budget and allocate project resources

2. Review project and provide authority to proceed at established management control points

3. Resolve problems whose scope exceeds the authority of task force members

THE TASK FORCE

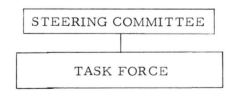

RULES FOR TASK FORCE

1. Composed of working level from departments concerned

2. Personnel meet as often as required

3. Call Steering Committee when necessary

4. Chairman from same department as chairman of Steering Committee

RESPONSIBILITIES OF TASK FORCE

1. Determine jointly with the Steering Committee which tasks should be accomplished for this project

2. Determine man-hours/dates/responsibility for tasks to be accomplished

3. Present plan to Steering Committee

4. Execute tasks

5. Present results to Steering Committee on routine basis

RESULTS OF THE STEERING COMMITTEE/ TASK FORCE STRUCTURE

The following significant results can be achieved for any project by following these simple rules and responsibilities.

* Top management (User & Data Processing) involvement is assured.

* Communication occurs on a routine, not a crisis, basis.

* The user is responsible for the resultant system.

* The task force has established channels to top management if they encounter project road blocks they cannot solve.

PURPOSE OF APPROACH

Simply stated, the purpose of the approach that I have described is such that the team workers, i.e., the task force, will know what management, i.e., the steering committee, expects; management has the opportunity to provide leadership and evaluate results. The ultimate purpose of this approach is to create an environment wherein management and project workers feel each has a <u>contract</u> with the other.

CONTINUOUS AUDIT

If an organization is to be successful in using a highly structured approach through published standards and procedures, there must be a continuous audit/training program. Use of a continuous audit also provides an opportunity to update standards and procedures as better methods are discovered. If there is no management commitment to the use of such comprehensive and expensive procedures, then the development and use of such procedures are surely not worth the price.

THE PROBLEMS AND POLITICS OF CHANGE:
POWER, CONFLICT, AND THE
INFORMATION SERVICES SUBUNIT

HENRY C. LUCAS, JR.

Graduate School of Business
Stanford University

INTRODUCTION

The most serious problems inhibiting the expansion and use of computer-based information systems are nontechnical in nature. In most organizations, the inability of users and Information Services personnel to work together to develop new systems and operate old ones has greatly diminished the utility of information systems. Many of these problems emanate from the change process which occurs when a new computer system is designed, implemented, and finally converted into normal production operations.

What is it about the nature of the Information Services subunit which results in these organizational problems? Why is the computer department any different from other subunits in the organization? In the following sections of the paper, the unique characteristics of the Information Services department will be shown to result in this subunit's accumulating a great deal of power in the organization, even though this may be unrecognized by most members of the organization. Power, combined with user frustration and lack of understanding of the technology, can easily lead to conflict. This conflict can drastically reduce the ability of the Information Services department to function and can have negative repercussions throughout the organization.

One of the most important activities of the Information Services department is designing and implementing new systems. It is maintained that this process is a type of planned change which is an important determinant of the relationship between Information Services and other subunits. The four major components of systems design are described and suggestions are offered for minimizing the problems created by this change effort.

THE ORGANIZATIONAL ENVIRONMENT OF THE INFORMATION SERVICES UNIT

A Theory of Organization Power

Recently, a theory of power has been elaborated which uses organizational subunits as the unit of analysis rather than individuals (6). The model stresses the relationship between the amount of organizational power and four variables: uncertainty, substitutability, workflow centrality, and the control of contingencies. Each of these variables will be discussed as it pertains to the relationship between the Information Services subunit and the rest of the organization.

Uncertainty

The model hypothesizes that the more a subunit in the organization copes with uncertainty, the more power it will have. Uncertainty is defined as the lack of information about future events which makes alternatives and outcomes less predictable. For operation or production systems such as billing and payroll applications, the user is dependent upon the operations section of the Information Services department to produce the required material accurately and on schedule. If schedules and standards are not consistently maintained, then there will be a great deal of uncertainty for the user on each run.

This uncertainty can not be reduced by the user; he must depend on the Information Services department to cope with it. To the extent that the user controlled the operation prior to the development of the computer system, the Information

Services department has created uncertainty for the user in developing a system. Thus, the Information Services department, by the nature of its activities, creates uncertainty for users with which only it can cope.

The Information Services department is also responsible for the production of information which is, itself, capable of reducing uncertainty for users. Examples of this information are sales histories, forecasts, and production control plans.

Substitutability

The second major variable in the power model is substitutability. It is hypothesized that the lower the substitutability of the activities of an organizational subunit, the greater its power. Most managements are unwilling to consider computer facilities that are not located and controlled within the organization itself. Management has always been afraid of having crucial data available outside of the physical confines of the organization. It is also difficult mechanically to substitute for the Information Services department. The computer area is notorious for poor documentation of systems and procedures, which reduces the possibility that a viable substitute to the status quo can be found. Thus, while substituting the services of an external service bureau or undertaking a facilities management arrangement are possible, they do not really constitute a serious threat to most Information Services departments.

Workflows

It is hypothesized that the higher the pervasiveness of workflows and the higher their immediacy, the greater the power of the subunit in the organization. Pervasiveness is defined as the degree to which the workflows of one department connect with workflows from others. The immediacy of workflows is the speed and severity with which they affect the outputs of the organization.

The pervasiveness of the workflows for the Information Services department varies according to the nature of the system. For production applications, such as billing, the

computer department may easily function as a critical link
in an assembly line which produces paper documents as physical products. For applications in which information is provided which is central to the operations of the organization,
the pervasiveness of the system will depend on the use of the
information. For example, inventory data are important,
but may not be as essential in reducing uncertainty or affecting output as a sales forecast.

The immediacy of the Information Services workflows also varies according to the application. Immediacy is extremely critical for an airline reservation system or for an
on-line inquiry system. The immediacy requirements of the
information processed may be less for other types of applications. However, for the typical organization, the workflows in the Information Services department will have above-
average immediacy.

Control of Contingencies

The power model hypothesizes that the more contingencies controlled by a subunit, the greater its power. This is
really a statement about the degree of interdependence between subunits. If unit A controls a large number of contingencies for unit B, then unit B is dependent upon unit A.
A mature Information Services department includes a number of applications across different areas and subunits in
the organization. It is this characteristic which makes the
Information Services department unique. It has more
contact and more impact on a variety of other people and
departments than most other departments. Other areas
which have contact with many departments, such as accounting or finance, are themselves frequently dependent upon
Information Services for processing.

Implications of Power

The power model is a multivariate relationship based
upon the four hypothesized relationships. As shown in the
figure, it is likely that feedback will occur so that increasing power will serve to reinforce itself, leading to the acquisition of even more power by a subunit. At this point in

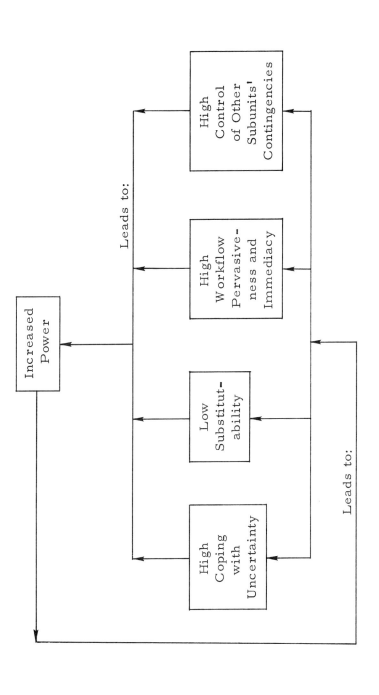

A POWER MODEL

time it is not clear how all of the four variables contribute to the total amount of power held by a subunit. However, the Information Services department rates highly on all of these variables and, therefore, can be expected to have much power. This high-power condition may not be understood by computer personnel. There is a tendency to look at each application individually and not examine the entire workflow of the Information Services department.

As a result of these conditions, the user may resent the surrender of some of his organizational power and the assignment of certain of his strategic contingencies to another department. This condition is exacerbated when the user does not understand the technology or the procedures involved. If the balance of power is inequitable, the results can be to encourage conflict between users and the Information Services subunit.

A CONFLICT MODEL

Conditions for Conflict

In addition to the power model described above, a conflict model has been proposed by Walton and Dutton (20). This model enumerates a number of conditions which can lead to conflict in an organization:

Mutual task dependence
Asymmetrical work relationships
Difference performance criteria and rewards
Differentiation
Role dissatisfaction
Ambiguities
Dependence on common resources
Communication obstacles
Personal skills and traits

The relationship between the Information Services department and other subunits in the organization has the potential for fulfilling all of these criteria. In discussing the power model, it was observed that the Information Services department increasingly controls strategic contingencies

for other subunits. In other words, these subunits will become more dependent on the Information Services department. Since information processing does depend on users
to supply input, correct errors, and assist in systems design (11) there will be high mutual task dependence. The
relationships between the computer area and other areas
are asymmetric because the computer professional must
understand the user's job where the reverse is not always
true.

Performance criteria differ; the reward structure for
users generally does not include any consideration of their
cooperation or participation in computer processing activities. Information Services personnel may be rewarded for
creativity or just installing a successful system.

The computer operation is a highly differentiated specialty; in fact, a different type of organizational structure
stressing creative workgroups may be the most appropriate
(3). An Information Services department which contains
loosely knit workgroups functioning at irregular hours may
be at odds with the structure of the rest of the organization.

The computer professional is often dissatisfied with his
role and with management. Both in the operation of existing
systems and in the design of new ones, there are many ambiguities. The responsibility for various activities and for
different problems is unclear. Errors are difficult to trace
and correct, and too frequently time is spent assigning
blame rather than creating a lasting solution to a problem.

Depending upon the budgeting process for Computer Services, there may be a dependence upon common resources
when it comes time to allocate funds. The Information Services unit may be seen as appropriating resources which
would otherwise have gone to user departments.

Communications obstacles between computer professionals and users are always pointed out as a continuing problem. There is a well-established computer jargon which
may compete with the jargon of the organization or the industry. Finally, the personal skills and traits of the computer professional differ from those of the users. One usually finds a different educational level and professional

orientation on the part of the computer specialist as distinct from the user.

Nature of Conflict

In certain circumstances conflict can be constructive; the notion of competition is an example of this. Frequently within an organization competitive teams and/or an advocacy approach are used to design systems. However, when conflict becomes destructive and results in internecine warfare, the results for the organization can be disastrous. The Information Services department and user departments are highly interdependent. The withholding of data, the return of incorrect computer runs, the refusal of interviews and materials during systems design can easily sabotage one department or the other. In fact, there is some evidence to suggest that it is not really possible to implement a system under conditions of extreme conflict.

IMPLICATIONS AND RESEARCH

Implications of the Models

The two models described above suggest that the Information Services department has a great deal of power in the organization and a potential for serious conflict with other subunits. In a situation where these conditions are not recognized, the Information Services department may tend to follow unsuccessful strategies in implementing new systems. The systems will be successful from a technical standpoint, but unsuccessful organizationally because they will create more conflict than existed previously. What can be done to make the transfer of power from users to the computer area more palatable and to reduce the level of conflict?

Research Findings

There have been very few studies which deal specifically with the unique situation of the Information Services department within the organization. In one study of 760 individuals representing users and computer professionals in six companies, conducted by the author, the results focused on four key variables in the relationship between the users and the Information Services subunit. Three of these variables are of interest here; they were found to be highly related to favorable attitudes towards the computer staff and/or ratings of high computer potential (see Table I). These three variables, in order of their importance, are: perceived quality

TABLE 1. PRELIMINARY RESEARCH RESULTS

Variables	Pearson Correlation*
Attitudes Towards the EDP Staff vs.	
Perceived Quality of Service	.50
Perceived Management Support	.34
Computer Potential	
Perceived Quality of Service	.40
Perceived Management Support	.29
Involvement	.22

*All values significant at the .05 level or better

of computer services, perceived management support, and involvement in systems design (11). This study suggests that all of these variables are interdependent and move together. That is, strong management support leads to more involvement in systems design, which increases the quality of service. Higher-quality computer service means more successful coping with uncertainty, which leads to more favorable user attitudes and a higher rating of computer potential. Thus, a cyclic relationship of increasingly favorable attitudes and dispositions towards the computer operation is established. It is also clear that a cycle moving in the opposite direction, though undesirable, is very possible.

Who is responsible for the control over these variables? While many different groups in the organization influence the variables, the primary responsibility can be assigned for each one. For the quality of computer services, the Information Services department is more influential, though user help is required. Management support must be furnished by the active involvement and participation of top

managers. Possible actions include modifying the reward
structure in order to compensate for successful information
processing systems, participation on committees, the assignment of users to work with the computer department,
and so on. Involvement, on the other hand, must be a joint
function of both users and the Information Services department. The computer professional must want to involve users, and users must be willing to spend time designing systems and working out the problems of existing systems.
This involvement must be meaningful so that suggestions
are fully considered and taken wherever advisable.

SYSTEMS DESIGN: A CRUCIAL ACTIVITY

Centrality of Systems Design

The activities of most Information Services departments
are divided into two major categories; the operation of existing systems and the design of new systems. Certainly, the
operation of existing systems is responsible for some of the
conflict conditions which arise over input and output, schedules, etc. However, the operation of a well-designed computer system is a production control management problem.
It may, on the other hand, be impossible to successfully operate a poorly designed computer system. Early computer
applications were primarily in the production area of billing
and payroll processing. As the industry has matured, more
information systems have been developed. As computer applications move into the areas of management control and
strategic planning, the systems design process becomes increasingly important in determining the future of the organization.

Systems design at the present time would have to be characterized as more of an art than a science. As experience
is gained, some of the technical aspects of systems design
are being conducted with more success. The state of knowledge about file structures has increased and more packaged
software is available than in the past, such as operating systems and data management facilities. There are still numerous problems in managing the technical development and

programming of a system, but it appears that in medium and small applications, these problems are beginning to be controlled. However, it is in the nontechnical areas of systems design where success has been much more limited. One of the major problems is the focus of the computer professional on the technical aspects of the system. Because his training concentrates upon these areas, the typical computer professional does not look at all of the implications of systems design.

Systems design should really be considered a process of planned change within the organization. The user department is transferring power to and becoming more interdependent with the Information Services department. Workflows are modified, and the content of various jobs changes. The change process encompasses both technological and human problems, which must receive equal attention. There are four major components which should be considered in the change process. The first is a technical one: How will the system actually perform? What is the nature of the information to be processed, what are the file structures, etc. ? This area is the mechanical or technological portion of the planned change activity.

The second major area of change is the impact on the user's task environment, which includes the incentives provided to cooperate with the system, the ease of I/O requirements, and the user's understanding of the system. The next major consideration in designing a system is its impact on the organization, which can be broken down into three subcomponents. The first is the impact on the organization itself, such as changes required among organizational subunits, and centralization and decentralization issues. The second type of impact occurs on work groups and the third on individuals. The fourth major component of the systems design-change activity is the actual process of designing the system and implementing it. This activity sets the tenor for the continued relationship between the user and the Information Services department. If the systems design process itself occurs in such a way as to increase conflict, these bad experiences will be very difficult to overcome during the operation of the system. The following sections of the paper discuss the research applicable to these four major components of systems design and the implications for improving systems design procedures.

The Mechanical Quality of Systems

Several general guidelines for systems design have been proposed by Ackoff (1). His first contention is that managers do not need more information; they suffer from an overabundance of irrelevant information now. The second suggestion is that giving a manager the information he needs may not improve decision making. These two contentions are supported by some experimental work (4) which has shown that people and groups have different optimum levels of information which they can successfully integrate in decision making. Unfortunately, the parameters are not yet known, but it appears that an extreme overload of information can lead to worse decision making. An individual is unable to cope with the information provided and therefore ignores potentially relevant sources in order to simplify the decision process.

Ackoff also maintains that managers may not know what they need; he calls for more explanatory models of decision making and information processing. It is suggested that instead of attempting to ask a manager about his information processing, the analyst should study the decision processes and the information flows which support these decisions. As computer applications move away from assembly line operations, such as billing and payments processing, into supporting managerial and strategic decisions, a decision-centered method of analysis will become more important.

These suggestions imply that the approach to systems design of blindly automating existing inputs and reports is not optimal. Even for paper-processing applications, changes in existing flows and tasks may be required. The mechanics of the system, combined with the physical interface discussed in the next section, determine the quality of EDP service. Technical elegance is undoubtedly less important to the user than the success of the system in fulfilling his perceived needs.

The System/Physical User Interface

In working with a new computer system, the user will probably have to make some changes in the structure of the tasks with which he is familiar. Such changes naturally raise anxieties on the part of the user, and it is important to design the physical interface to minimize the inconvenience. Some of the specific problems which irritate users have been enumerated along with suggested solutions (21). First, it is extremely important to make the system as flexible and easy to change as possible. One of the most common complaints about computer systems is their rigidity; it is important to recognize that any system, even after conversion, is in a fluid and dynamic state as experience is gained using it.

It is also suggested that obscure codes for input and output and mysterious procedures will contribute to the frustration of the user. For on-line systems it is recommended that silent printing terminals or CRT's be used to minimize the physical objections to the terminal device. Wherever possible function keys, overlays, and menu selection techniques should be used to minimize the input requirements, since most users will probably not be accomplished typists. In early systems the cost for these more sophisticated terminals was prohibitive; however, with today's technology there is very little excuse for not using them.

Technology has also helped to make storage costs lower so that it is not unreasonable to use courteous and fully explanatory messages when errors do occur. When designing messages, it is useful for the analyst to place himself in the position of the user. An error message should serve a training function and should provide feedback which can be used to improve the user's performance. Error messages which cannot be understood or which denigrate the user's intelligence should be avoided.

Because the design of this portion of the system is so crucial in providing an incentive for the system to be used, two suggestions can be made for a general approach following the specification of requirements (13). First, a supreme effort should be made to pretest the system before actual conversion. It is recognized that implementing a new system will show bugs not caught in testing. However, it seems fairly obvious that the fewer of these errors which occur, the more readily the system will be accepted. One technique which has been used in the past is to assign a separate group who are not cognizant of the internal functionings of the system to prepare inputs for testing which attempt to cause the system to fail. A second suggestion is to try out the system experimentally before conversion. Software is tested routinely to be sure that it accomplishes the objectives stated in the program specifications; however, it is also important to test the user interface. Before the specifications are frozen, it is a good idea to try experiments with users to determine if the design is feasible from their standpoint. Prior to implementation, the actual system itself should be field tested, preferably on a group who will actually use it. It is just as important to design the physical interface well as it is to successfully develop the program modules.

Impact on the Organization

It is this component of the systems design process which is the most frequently omitted. The results of the omission can be unanticipated changes in the organization or unanticipated responses on the part of the individuals who must use the system. Rather than ex post facto analysis of what happened, it is possible to forecast and plan for the impact of a system on three different levels: the organization itself, workgroups, and individuals.

Organization Level. On the organizational level, Ackoff has suggested that one fallacy in systems design has been the idea that more communications lead to better performance (1). This certainly is not true according to the conflict model if organizational subunits are experiencing a high level of conflict. If the Information Services department places itself in the position of a link between two departments under high conflict, then problems can be expected. The information provided from a computer system can be used to increase the level of conflict and give one subunit the upper hand over another. The Information Services department then becomes a central link in a win/lose situation (2). Under such conditions it may be necessary to postpone the design

of the technical system until the organizational problems can
be solved. Such problems are generally not within the competence of the Information Services department to resolve,
but require the use of specialists in organizational development or possibly sensitivity training (7).

Another example of the potential organizational impact of
a computer system is in the much discussed area of centralization vs. decentralization. If centralization is defined as
the locus of decision-making responsibility, then it is clear
that the information systems of an organization will have a
major impact on centralization or decentralization. The impact depends upon where information is provided and to
whom the responsibility for a decision is assigned. Early
questions in this field arose as to whether the computer
would lead to more centralization or not (10). Centralization or decentralization should be viewed as an independent
variable which is under the control of the systems design
process, not as a dependent variable to be examined after
implementation. Systems designers should consider where
the information is provided for current decision making and
how it is to be provided under the new system. Do the information flows and locations for decision making corre-
spond with management goals for centralization and decentralization?

Work Groups. Following a thorough analysis of the impact of the system on the structure of the organization, the
impact on workgroups should be considered. There has been
a great deal of literature in the organization behavior area
which discusses the importance of the social rewards which
come from a worker's peer group. Examples have been
cited of using group planning to reorganize workflows and to
make technical changes. Where the group is actually involved in the decisions leading to the changes, greater productivity has been the result (see the discussion of participation in the next section). The importance of regarding the
workgroup as a "socio-technical system" has been stressed;
a group cannot be viewed as just a vehicle for production (16,
19). Even though many of the studies in the literature have
been of factory workers, it seems reasonable to generalize
the findings to clerical workers and many information

processing jobs. The computer system often changes the
task procedures, and may even change the basic structure
of the workgroup. Are these changes necessary? Is it possible to use the workgroup itself to decide how to cope with
these changes and restructure the task? It is important
again to try and forecast any changes and to plan for them.

Individuals. The final level of the analysis of the impact
of a computer system on the organization is the individual
himself. Moving from group level forecasts of change,
Mumford and Ward (14) advocate detailed planning for the
potential impact of a system on each individual. They suggest it is important to try and anticipate the positive and
negative aspects of changes that will be created by the system. What attitudes are involved, what portions of the system are most susceptible to change, and what is the probable
reaction for each individual? It may be simple to change
some part of the technical design or system flows to reduce
the impact on different individuals. If system changes are
not possible, it has been found that employees react dif-
ferently to systems based on age, sex, and position in the
organization. Therefore, different approaches to change
are appropriate for different individuals. Mumford and
Ward (14) provide a detailed example of such forecasting on
the individual level.

Systems Design Process

The final component of systems design which needs to be
examined is the process of design itself. The way in which
systems design is undertaken and its success will set the
tone of the relationship between users and the Information
Services subunit. This process begins at the initial request
for a feasibility study and continues through the final implementation and conversion of the system. A number of au-
thors suggest that involvement and participation are important aspects of systems design. The historical foundations
for this participation and group decision making were established in studies by Lewin and by Coch and French (15).
These latter two researchers found in a factory situation that
a group which participated in altering their tasks achieved

higher productivity after the change than groups with no participation. In another setting, Lawler and Hackman (8), found that the goals of an incentive pay plan were more nearly obtained by groups that had participated in the development of the plan than by groups where the plan had been imposed or no plan at all had been developed. The interesting aspect of this study was that even with a 60% turnover, the norm established by the participative groups was perpetuated and adhered to by the new employees a year later (17).

Taking these findings into account, a method has been suggested by the author (11) to use questionnaires and interviews to gather design data and attitudinal responses in developing computer systems. The design data can be used for the mechanical component of the design process while the attitudinal data can be used to help plan implementation, forecast the impact of the system on workgroups and individuals, and sensitize the systems design personnel. Repeated monitoring through various stages of the project is also suggested. Though the concept has not been completely tested, there is some evidence of its efficacy (12). (The use of the attitudinal data is somewhat similar to the feedback methods of organizational change proposed by Floyd Mann (7).)

One of the most important aspects of user involvement is considering the participants' responses fully. If a suggestion is not taken, efforts should be made to explain why so that the reasons are understood and accepted. Pseudo-participation in which information is solicited and not considered is certainly worse than no participation at all and will lead to heightened conflict with users.

One of the major reasons for encouraging participation in the design process and in workgroup and individual changes is that involvement helps the individual to become more committed to the plan and more knowledgeable about it. Ackoff has also suggested that managers must understand systems in order to be able to use them (1). Participation is one method to create exposure to systems and to increase the level of understanding. There is also some evidence that genuine participation will help users develop more trust in the Information Services department (8).

In order to reduce some user frustration, it is helpful for the Information Services department to have representatives to whom the user can turn in times of stress. This may require special liaison personnel, steering committees, or other devices to help encourage participation. It is also desirable to continue participation during the operation of existing systems as well as systems design. The survey techniques advocated for designing a system can be extended to monitoring the user interface with production systems. Attitudes towards presently operating systems will help to assess the nature of the relationship between users and systems. Design questions can be used to obtain suggestions for modifying existing systems and procedures. This involvement and participation will combine with management support and improved quality of service and, hopefully, lead to an increasingly favorable relationship between the Information Services department and the user.

Conclusions

The recommendations for actions for each of the four components of system design are summarized in Table 2. This strategy emphasizes a viewpoint of systems design as an organizational process of planned change. Certainly, purely technical problems of coding, debugging, and program testing are also important, but there is a large body of literature dealing with these problems. Many systems have achieved less than their full potential because of the failure to consider all of the aspects of systems design.

The transfer of power from users to the Information Services department and the changes in workflows clearly make the design and implementation of an information system an organizational change. Therefore, if successful systems are to be developed, more than the mechanical portion of the system will have to be taken into account. It is contended that the mechanics of the system are just one component and that the physical user interface, the potential impact of the system on the organization, and the process of systems design deserve at least equal attention.

TABLE 2. SYSTEMS DESIGN AND PLANNED CHANGE

Components of Systems Design	Recommendations
1. Mechanical Quality of System	a. Provide filtered information b. Do not overload with data c. Examine decisions and data flows d. Be sure the system works!
2. Physical User Interface	a. Design for flexibility b. Use understandable error codes; be polite c. Provide educational feedback d. Use appealing terminals e. Experiment with interface f. Test exhaustively; implement gradually
3. Impact on the Organization 3.1 Entire Organization	a. Consider relations (conflict level) among subunits b. Consider impact on locus of decision-making responsibility
3.2 Work Groups	c. Examine task as "sociotechnical" system d. Avoid reassigning successful work groups e. Encourage group participation in changing tasks
3.3 Individuals	f. Forecast impact on individuals g. Modify system and/or develop implementation strategy h. Encourage participation in changes

TABLE 2 (Cont'd.)

Components of Systems Design	Recommendations
4. Process of Design	a. Encourage participation with user surveys
	b. Establish representatives to work with user
	c. Incorporate user suggestions into design

SUMMARY

A model of power distribution among organizational sub-units was applied to the conditions existing between the Information Services department and the rest of the organization. It was concluded that the process of developing systems results in the transfer of power to the computer department, which can cause frustrations for the user and increase the level of conflict between the computer professional and the user. A second model dealing with conflict was also applied to the relationship between users and the Information Services department and it showed that numerous conditions leading to conflict were present in the relationship. Next, research findings were explored which showed three key variables which are associated with favorable attitudes towards the computer staff and ratings of computer potential. These include high-quality computer service, management support, and involvement in the design of new systems.

The importance of systems design was stressed for determining the quality of systems and readying users to work with the Information Services department. Research findings and recommendations were reviewed for four major components of systems design, including the mechanical parts of the system, the physical user interface, the organizational impact, and the systems design process itself.

It was stressed that the organizational impact should be considered from the standpoint of the entire organization and its subunits. Workgroups and their tasks should be considered as a "socio-technical system," and the impact on each individual in the organization needs to be examined. It was recommended from historical studies that the process of systems design itself could be improved through participation, and a method for eliciting participation using questionnaires and interviews was recommended.

It is hoped that attention to these four major components of systems design will help to reduce conflict and minimize the adverse effects of the power transfers inherent in designing new systems. These techniques should facilitate both the short- and long-range success of the changes in the organization brought about by the design of new information systems.

REFERENCES

1. Ackoff, R. L. , "Management Misinformation Systems, " Management Science, 14, no. 4, (December 1967), pp. B147-B156.

2. Argyris, Chris, "Management Information Systems: The Challenge to Rationality and Emotionality, " Management Science, 17, no. 6, (February 1971), pp. B275-B292.

3. Becker, S. and N. Baloff, "Organizational Structure and Complex Problem Solving, " Administrative Science Quarterly, 14, no. 2, (June 1969), pp. 260-271.

4. Driver, M. and S. Streufert, "Interpretive Complexity: An Approach to Individuals and Groups as Information Processing Systems, " Administrative Science Quarterly, 14, no. 2, (June 1969), pp. 272-285.

5. Glaser, George, "Commitment. . . . the Unreachable Star ?" Datamation, 17, no. 11, (June 1, 1971), pp. 38-41.

6. Hickson, P. J. , C. R. Hennings, C. A. Lee, R. E. Schneck, and J. M. Pennings, "A Strategic Contingencies Theory of Interorganizational Power, " Administrative Science Quarterly, 16, no. 2, (June 1971), pp. 216-229.

7. Katz, D. and R. L. Kahn, The Social Psychology of Or-
    ganizations. New York: John Wiley and Sons, Inc.,
    1966.

8. Lawler, E. E., III and R. J. Hackman, "Impact of Em-
    ployee Participation in the Development of Pay Incen-
    tive Plans: A Field Experiment," Journal of Applied
    Psychology, 53, no. 6, (December 1969), pp. 467-
    471.

9. Lawrence, P. R. and J. W. Lorsch, Organizations and
    Environment. Boston: Division of Research, Gradu-
    ate School of Business Administration, Harvard Uni-
    versity, 1967.

10. Leavitt, H. and T. Whisler, "Management in the 1980's,"
    Harvard Business Review, November-December
    1958, pp. 41-48.

11. Lucas, H. C., Jr., "A User-Oriented Approach to Sys-
    tems Design," Proceedings: 1971 ACM Annual Con-
    ference, pp. 325-338.

12. _____, "The Development of an Information System
    for a Voluntary Organization," Stanford University,
    Graduate School of Business Working Paper No. 191R,
    1971.

13. McCracken, D. D., "...but the Ambivalence Lingers,"
    Datamation, 17, no. 1, (January 1, 1971), pp. 29-30.

14. Mumford, E. and T. B. Ward, Computers: Planning for
    People. London. B. T. Batsford Ltd, 1968.

15. Proshansky, H. and B. Seidenberg (eds.), Basic Studies
    in Social Psychology. New York: Holt, Rinehart and
    Winston, 1965.

16. Rice, A. K., Productivity and Social Organization; the
    Ahmedabad Experiment. London: Tavistock Publica-
    tions, Ltd., 1958.

17. Scheflen, K. C., E. E. Lawler, III, and R. J. Hackman, "Long-Term Impact of Employee Participation in the Development of Pay Incentive Plans: A Field Experiment Revisited," Journal of Applied Psychology, 55, no. 3, (June 1971), pp. 182-186.

18. Thompson, J. D., Organizations in Action. New York: McGraw-Hill Book Company, 1967.

19. Trist, E. L., Organizational Choice. London: Tavistock Publications Ltd., 1963.

20. Walton, R. E. and J. M. Dutton, "The Management of Interdepartmental Conflict: A Model and Review," Administrative Science Quarterly, 14:73-84, (March 1969).

21. Withington, F. G., "Cosmetic Programming," Datamation, 16, no. 3, (March 1970), pp. 91-95.

DESIGN PRINCIPLES FOR THE
MATURING PROFESSION

ROBERT L. PATRICK

Computer Specialist
Northridge, California

Let me begin by qualifying myself as a computer expert.
I'm a graduate mechanical engineer and I've been active in
computing for 21 years, 13 of which have been spent as an
independent consultant. My present clients include the IBM
Corporation, Hughes Aircraft, the Los Angeles Times,
System Development Corporation, and Bekins. My past
work has included data reduction, engineering design, and
simulation, market research, on-line commercial systems,
and real-time business applications. In the software area,
I am a co-designer of IMS/360, which is an IBM package for
handling on-line data bases, and which runs on top of OS/360.
In the area of hardware, I worked on the Burroughs 5000,
the TRW 530, and was the only outsider on the architectural
team for the 360 itself. I have done extensive work in the
management area, performing technical audits, reorganiza-
tions, job descriptions, and proposal writing. I'm not a
particularly good coder any more; they hire me because of
the breadth of my experience.

I think that the range of my work qualifies me to discuss
the effective use of computers on large-scale projects. I'd
like to focus attention on systems where the public has a
large third-party interest, such as law enforcement systems, voting systems, and credit reporting systems. These
are systems that are visible; they are systems that are
most in need of design principles.

In the 1950's the computer field went through a juvenile stage in which we picked off applications that were well defined, largely self-contained, and that had a guaranteed high yield.

The 1960's were our adolescent years, in which we gleefully tried a large variety of things, some of which were successful. But many of the things we tried were not cost-effective.

We're now in the young adulthood stage in the 1970's. Dollars are tight, and we're having to learn how to manage properly, to meet our schedules, and to deliver the function we promised within budget and on time.

I like to explain the term "information system" by showing people a chart, some 35 feet long, that defines such a system, one that produces illustrated parts catalogs for jet aircraft. A parts catalog shows a detailed picture of some portion of an airplane on one page and on the facing page lists all the parts numbers and subassemblies. The 35-foot flow diagram describes the steps that produce such a catalog; these steps control the work of 82 full-time people, not including computer people. The process chart dictates, for the production of one parts catalog, the use of 30 hours of 360/50 time; 330 hours of 360/30 time; the accessing of 136 distinct files (ranging from 3 x 5 card files to reels of computer tape); and 564 process blocks (ranging from filling in a checklist, to a listing pass on a 360/30). Such a system is the typical information system of the 1970's, where man-machine interaction is the key. In my opinion, the days are gone in which a single program could be considered equivalent to a single system. The particular system chart that I refer to represents 120 man-days of work and cost about $10,000. The chart was produced in order to analyze and improve a complex system that had evolved over some years and which was only dimly understood by the people who used it. As a by-product, we produced a manual to describe how to produce such charts. Thus, our analysis techniques are keeping pace with our system design needs.

Let me try to define the computing profession—a conglomerate of people and machines that is now beginning to congeal and show some signs of maturity. We are beginning to work on codes of ethics, and our fantastic salary progression is now leveling off.

Let's look at where we are. Consider the vocabulary area: our success at defining our terms. The American National Standard Vocabulary for Information Processing is just out. It is abominably poor, and costs $6. It took too long to produce; it lacks many of the current terms of the field; and in my opinion, it is just a big mistake.

In the area of standards for programming and systems, they are simply nonexistent. We keep trying to develop standards with part-time help, and no one thinks to ask why those people should have the time to develop standards. The development of useful standards requires knowledgeable and competent people, and they deserve to be paid. We seem to be busy setting standards for the second generation, but my clients are pushing into the fourth generation.

There are specific standards efforts that are pretty good. I might cite the standards manual developed by the Chemical Abstracts Service of Columbus, Ohio, for their own use. One thing that makes it different is that the text is contained on a computer to make it easy to keep it current. This appears to be a simple and obvious device; why did it take us twenty years to think of it? If a set of standards isn't current, then it is already obsolete, and programmers will quickly reject it.

Let's look at our training programs. We have some good ones, but by and large this area is spotty. Just for example, consider the UCLA catalog of courses in computer science. It contains courses like

Computerized Structural Analysis.

Computer Analysis of Networks.

Computer Applications in Combinatorial Mathematics.

Recent Advances in Computer Communications.

Computer Communication Transport and Switching Networks.

Numerical Analysis and Digital Computer Methods in Engineering.

Management Information Systems.

Computer Systems Modeling.

Operating Systems.

These are probably all fine courses, but from my point of view it makes for a spotty coverage of the problems my clients face. If I want to improve my grasp of the field, I don't think it would be useful to study all existing operating systems, and even less useful to learn about all the programming languages that have been invented. The academic world, it seems to me, needs to pay some attention to the problems out in the real world.

We are now starting to get some good books in our field. Management Information Systems Handbook by Hartman, et al. is a good reference on project systems analysis and management. Let me commend Joseph Orlicky's book, The Successful Computer System, written to your boss's reading level. He's the guy you have to convince, on many topics, and anything that can improve your communication with him is worth it. Orlicky has written a book that can do a world of good for a chief engineer, or a controller, or a vice president of marketing—people who may be scared of computers. They're scared because they don't even understand enough about computers to argue with you when you say you need a 10% increase in your budget. I recommend that the next time you intend to make a pitch for a big new project, you educate your boss about six months ahead of time with this book.

We are behind the times in this country in the area of guidelines and codes of ethics. The British are ahead of us. The British Computer Society has published a Code of Good Practice, about 30 pages long, which adds up to a good start. I would hope that the corresponding U.S. societies would follow suit.

Let me turn to the law. At the local level, there is little in the laws that affects computer people. Anyone can be a consultant, for example, by buying a business license; there are no tests to pass, no sanctions on his conduct, and no body of knowledge that he has to demonstrate. He can get on a dozen lists of bidders for government contracts simply by knocking on a few doors; there are no stated qualifications.

There is even less at the state level. There is no mechanism for licensing or regulating computer people, although there has been some talk about it.

At the federal level, governmental agencies are worried about only two things relating to computers. One is privacy, chiefly that of the government's data banks. The other is monopoly, which is chiefly a worry of the courts.

Our industry is beginning to learn how to write job specifications, which shows progress of a sort. We can define in detail what a "Microform Planner" should know (see Figure 1), so that we can avoid one of the common mistakes of

Job Description:

Microform Planner

Skill Number	Skill	Emphasis Units
1	Microforms Knowledge	50
2	Standards for Microforms Development	50
3	Planning for Microforms Development	50
4	Organized Microform Awareness Files	50
5	Organized Microform Expert's Files	50
6	General Systems Analysis Skills	50
7	Specific Systems Analysis Skills Involving On-Line Files and Inquiry	50
8	Project Administration	10
9	Project Management	10
10	Project Costing and Estimating	10
11	Programming	5
12	Coding	5
13	Debugging	5
14	On-Going Operations	5
	Total	400

FIGURE 1

the past; namely, moving a software SYSGEN specialist into a slot on the organization chart simply because he could spell "microfiche."

We are getting manuals of system design, but most of these are parochial (we lack broad segments of knowledge), and all of them could not be updated for new equipment without essentially redoing all the work.

There is little progress that I can see in implementation and testing; we're still using the tools and methods of ten to fifteen years back. There doesn't seem to be money available for the purpose, and money is what it takes to make a field congeal.

In the area of installation and evaluation, there has been some work done in component evaluation, but very little in systems evaluation. I was involved in a hardware system evaluation at North American Rockwell some years ago. There were 21 men on the team, half from North American and half from IBM, measuring the effectiveness of a room full of 360's. We had performance monitors tied to the machines, and plotters to plot our observations. The entire effort was in contrast to the claims you see in the ads, for which someone offers to tie a gadget to your machine and tell you in a day how well you're operating. Diagnosis made that quickly will be about as good as a medical checkup that is made quickly. If a medical diagnosis is any good, it involves some lab tests and more measurements made after the lab tests return, and a detailed discussion with the doctor.

Of course, you want to measure and count the obvious things: CPU usage, and peripheral device usage, and whether you have everything for which you're paying rent, and whether you're using the devices you're renting. The evaluation at North American involved three weeks of measurements (three shifts for 21 days) and cost $90,000. The installation at that time had three model 65's, one model 50, and many model 30's.

I'm running through the list of things that contribute to maturity in the field. As far as costing and estimating are concerned, I detect no progress in the last fifteen years. We need a breakthrough in this area. Many large projects

are started with estimates so poor that the project is over
its budget from the first day—and doesn't know it. Despite
what must be by now a large mass of data, we are still no-
toriously poor at estimating the costs of any computing project.

We're doing much better in the area of project management. The big software houses and all the major manufacturers have project management handbooks, and they're
pretty good. The accumulated knowledge has been recorded
and is available to those who need it.

Assuming that we can get a big system created and tested, where do we stand on systems operation? Some guidelines for good systems operation are appearing. IBM has a
course in it with fair content, and there are seminars being
given that are not bad.

It's about the same with systems management. It's beginning to be reduced to a set of clear guidelines, even
though not many people are following them.

In the area of long-range planning, we're in bad shape.
For most installations, they'll be in good shape if they can
just get through the next month-end closing. They don't
know how they got through the last year-end closing (when
the weekly, monthly, quarterly, and annual reports are all
needed at once), and they fear the next one. I have seen a
written history of such a year-end closing for a large financial shop. I can't help wondering, considering how many
such adventures there have been, why it took so long for
someone to write it down. Our long-range planning efforts
are simply nil. We don't have any idea of how to express
the relations between standards, business growth, budgets,
and planning for computer-based systems.

Listed in Figure 2 is the matrix of the secondary characteristics of computer systems. I do most of my work in
the area of private systems, such as an internal management reporting system. For such systems, particularly
large ones, the integrity is weak. Integrity refers to the
ability of the system to hold up, day after day, without losing chunks of a file, or a disk index. Does the accuracy of
the output tend to deteriorate over time? In the systems
I've worked with, the answer is yes. Integrity is hard to

Matrix of Secondary System Characteristics
Where We Stand

	Internal Management Information and Reporting System Private Systems	Law Enforcement Government Systems	Subscription Credit Management Quasi-Public Systems	Vote Counting Public Systems
Integrity	Hard to establish & hard to hold with on-line data bases	Unknown; no audits; some symptoms of trouble	Barely acceptable	Poor
Reliability/Availability	Simple systems O.K.; complex systems push art	Ditto	Acceptable	Fair
Quality	Acceptable	Ditto; occasional court case	Mediocre	Poor
Cost	High	Buried in confusing budgets	High; requires multiple subscribers	O.K.
Security and Privacy	Primitive	Very sensitive; needs federal regulations	Visually O.K. internally fair	Fair
Control of Operations	Complex systems at fringe of art	Barely adequate	Probably O.K. (complexity medium)	Poor
Management of Change	Just beyond art	Beyond art	Just beyond art	Poor
Examples	Airlines, O.K.; big industry just fair	LAPD hidden; drivers license good	Computer Credit & TRW Credit Data-- much mystery; design questionable; some errors	Complexity undiscovered; costly panic efforts to solve

FIGURE 2

establish, and harder to maintain when you're dealing with on-line data bases.

For reliability and availability, we do quite well for small, simple systems. For large, complex systems, we're pushing the state of the art to the limit.

If we can get such systems under control, the quality is acceptable and the cost is high. The security and privacy is primitive. Control of the operation is at the fringes of the art. The management of change is beyond our present capability. We design and implement large systems, only to find that a one-digit change in one field calls for major reworking of the programs.

About the only large on-line systems that can be said to work well are the airlines reservations systems; the airlines have faced up to the problems and allocate large amounts of money to their solution. Similar systems in other industries are, at best, only fair.

So much for private systems; now look at governmental systems, such as those used in law enforcement. The integrity of such systems is unknown to the outsider, but there are symptoms that indicate that there are troubles. The problems are the same as those in industrial systems, but government employees are paid much less and are known to go home at 5:00 on Fridays, whereas their industrial counterparts don't. The reliability and availability in governmental systems is probably poor (again, it's difficult for an outsider to find out) and the quality, or lack of it, shows up in lawsuits by people who assert that the systems have maligned them. The cost is unknown, since all costs are buried in layers of interlocking budgets.

I suspect that the security and privacy of the government systems I have seen is weak, but difficult to determine. I doubt that it will be improved without federal regulation. Their control of the operation of the system is barely adequate, and the management of change is beyond the state-of-the-art.

An example of quasi-public systems is the credit bureaus; I call them subscription credit management systems. The two leaders in this locale are TRW Credit DATA and Computer Credit Corporation. The integrity of these

systems is barely acceptable. The Fair Credit Reporting
Act of 1971 required such firms to disclose to any individual the content of their files relating to him. They may, and
do, impose a nuisance charge for doing this. I went to both
local firms to obtain the data on me, and the results are interesting. For one thing, they give you an unformatted
printout of the record, and a counselor aids you in inter-
preting the codes used. The law was intended to protect an
individual's rights, but such laws must obviously be rewrit-
ten by someone who knows something about computing.
They were trying to protect the poor and the ignorant, but
to little avail if someone who has been in the computing field
for 21 years can't decipher the printout.

By working patiently at it, I could do some unscrambling,
since I could locate my various credit account numbers and
I knew the amounts of my recent transactions. But then I
found significant items (that is, items that should be significant) glaringly absent. For instance, neither company
noted my ownership of a home or of two cars, which may not
be important, except that I'm asked for just that information
whenever I apply for credit. They had my credit car numbers correct, but one of them had my social security number wrong!

After officially contacting one credit agency, I got a tour
of their facility and found they had in fact printed out all the
information they knew about me; it's just that they knew very
little. I discovered that the credit agencies are at the mer-
cy of the cooperating subscribers in building their data
bases. All the credit agency does is to take the data that is
offered up by the subscribers, organize it, and feed it back
out to the other subscribers for a fee—a clearing house operation. Thus since most of the credit subscribers fail to
keyboard home ownership, automobile registration, education, or background from the credit application, it's not
available in the subscriber system and hence doesn't pass
through the clearing house. I was surprised to find they
had social security numbers on only 38% of the records.
No wonder they have trouble mating the correct credit history with the proper person.

While their credit data bases do carry both positive and

negative information on individuals and while they are attempting to assist the credit grantor in dispensing credit to
worthy applicants, it just seems a very funny way to run a
business when the subscribers are in control of the basic
content of the data base.

Their reliability and availability must be all right, since
they are still in business and I haven't been turned down for
credit. Judging by my one sample, I was not impressed
with their quality. The system cost is high, which is why
the credit business exists; few firms can afford their own
credit systems. Their security looks all right (there are
guards at hand, for example) but I doubt that their people
are properly cleared or bonded. Their data moves uncrypt-
ed over telephone lines. It seems to me that their security
is largely for show.

Operations control for the credit systems is probably
good, because the system is basically simple with one dedicated machine running on-line continuously. Such systems
can be settled down with reasonable expectation of having
them remain stable. (Big systems with foreground on-line
processing and variegated batch processing in background
are much more difficult to settle down.)

Other governmental systems are those maintained by the
state for motor vehicle records, and local vote counting
systems. From my observations, the state is in better
shape than the credit bureaus. For fifty cents, I was able
to obtain a printout of my driver's record and it seemed to
be accurate, up to date, and readable.

The local vote counting systems are considerably worse.
The integrity is poor; the systems are simply badly designed.
I was involved in an audit of an election in Los Angeles in
which, six weeks after the election, they could not balance
their figures against the precinct totals. The availability of
vote counting systems is weak; the record is held by Fresno,
where for one election the computer program was not ready
for production until three days after the election. The quality is poor; they are unable to furnish ordinary management
statistics and they can't maintain normal accounting controls
on the number of ballots. The cost is all right, since it
competes with thousands of people counting complicated

ballots by hand. Security is better than it used to be (they now keep the tourists out of the machine room while vote counting is taking place), but still weak.

Operations control in vote counting is fair, and at every election it is touch and go whether things will be ready in time. As far as management of change goes, that phrase is unknown to the people who designed the system. It is complicated by California law, which requires that the position of names on the ballots be rotated, so that every candidate has an equal chance of being at the top of his section of the ballot for some precincts. Even so, it should be possible to generate ballot arrangements from tables stored in the system, but that is not the case. They are only now discovering the inherent complexity of vote counting, but it leads to costly panic efforts at solution.

I've mentioned complexity. In Figure 3, we see the relation between computer power and related cost. This is related to Grosch's Law; as you increase size, you can expect some benefits from the economies of scale. In computing work, when your computing power doubles, the cost does not quite double. When you go from one unit of computing to two units, your cost may go from 100 to 175 or so. The chart shows these relations, but that's only part of the picture. There are many other factors, which is what I've been trying to describe.

Computer Power vs. Complexity

Financial View		Practical Considerations	
Computer Power	Related Cost	Support Costs	System Complexity*
1	100	1	1.0
2	175	2	2.5
4	300	3	8.0
8	450	4	20.0

*For general purpose workloads with teleprocessing

FIGURE 3

For example, there are support costs. A shop with an
IBM 7094 would have five or six full-time professional systems programmers, at $15,000 per year each (direct labor
cost). When you go to a 370/165 (which is about eight times
the computer power of the 7094), you might need 40 systems
programmers. The troubles and costs of system support
(those men, plus the machine time they consume) go up about
linearly with the computing power.

If you are maintaining an uncomplicated workload (like
the famous Los Alamos jobs where you read one card in the
morning, grind away all day, and print one line in the after-
noon), then the complexity stays constant and it pays to get
bigger and bigger machines. But where you run a job mix of
scientific and commercial work, with some on-line data-
base jobs, and teleprocessing, and text processing—then the
complexity increases exponentially as you go to larger machines. We have gone up by a factor of eight in machine
power, but I don't think we can double it again. We are already at the point where the collection of OS/360 manuals is
bigger than one man can read, much less absorb. We are
simply intellectually awash with the complexity of today's
technology.

Many organizations have not yet reached that factor of
eight, and I believe that they aren't going to. The law enforcement agencies are proposing to interconnect all the law
enforcement systems in the country by telephone lines; I can
only hope that Ma Bell prevents it from working. The systems analysts that they depend on, and the contractors they
deal with, are just not capable of moving into that level of
complexity.

The city of Los Angeles has a Wants and Warrants file,
on-line, whereby the name of a person who is apprehended
for any reason can be submitted to the file according to
standard identifying criteria to see if he is wanted. The Los
Angeles people are pretty careful to maintain the quality of
the data in their file. But their system is linked to a state-
wide system that is, in turn, linked to other states, and not
everyone is as careful about the quality of his data; thus, the
links tend to degrade the loqal data base. These things are
going to get worse, since eager computer salesmen and

software experts urge agencies to plug their systems together, without insisting on the checks and balances that are
needed when you go from a system of complexity 2 and make
a new system of complexity 4.

I'd like to indicate the direction I think we should go and
how I think we ought to get there. First, I think we need a
good glossary of terms in our field, plus the mechanism to
keep it current. We do not now have definitions of terms
that are adequate in contracts, in multivendor negotiations,
and in courts of law. Just for an example, the recent ANSI
glossary doesn't mention "read-only memory," a term that
began in 1964. I've tried for years to stir up interest in a
good glossary, but I have failed to get any group turned on
over the idea.

We need to evolve a body of preferred practice drawn
from the best that is now done. AFIPS has a systems certification committee at work, as an outgrowth of some work-
shop sessions held in 1971. Previously, some efforts were
made in California to establish machinery for state registration and certification of people. I suggested to them that
it might be better to try to certify systems, rather than
people. This idea took root and, as a result of the AFIPS
project, we may soon see the first book of standard practice.

We need to separate out those systems in which the public has a third-party interest (such as law enforcement,
credit, and voting systems) and establish guidelines for
them. We need to be able to certify such systems prior to
their use, but we can't do that without some guidelines (and
I believe it would be difficult to establish guidelines without
a glossary). We must arrange to recertify such systems
every time they're changed, and that will require change
boards that can act very promptly.

If that can be achieved, then we can hope that private
systems will adopt the best guidelines for internal use.

Each individual, if he agrees these goals are worthy, can
aid the effort in several ways. You can write articles for
and letters to our trade magazines. You can work within
your professional societies, either to foster the endeavors
now under way, or to instigate better ones.

Panel Discussion

THE ROLE OF EDUCATION IN PREPARING
EFFECTIVE COMPUTING PERSONNEL

Moderator

Fred Gruenberger

Professor
School of Business and Economics
California State University, Northridge

Panelists

Curtis F. Gerald

Head, Computer Science and Statistics Dept.
California State Polytechnic University
San Luis Obispo

Richard W. Reynolds
Associate Professor, Business Administration Division
Orange Coast College

118

Prof. Gruenberger

The members of this panel are teachers of computing.
It is our job to supply the computing world with young people
who are trained and educated in the techniques and skills of
a fast-changing industry.

We cannot function statically. We must continually seek
feedback from the real world of computing in order to try to
teach the subject as it exists and, hopefully, to get some
feel for how it will exist when our students get out there.

To this end, I ask managers of working installations what
it is they want from us. What sort of a product should we
produce? By and large, the answer I get boils down to this:
each man wants new hires who are just like him. This is
understandable, but overlooks the fact that the manager got
where he is after twenty years of experience and study (frequently tracing back to punched card techniques), and he expects us to perform this transmogrification in about eight-
een months. Even allowing for the fact that today's students
have better teachers (that's not immodest; twenty years ago
there were few teachers of the subject at all, and no text-
books), it's asking for a lot. The manager also tends to
overlook, or forget, the picture that he presented as an
undergraduate. If you have saved any of your college papers,
you would probably not want anyone to see them now.

It has been my experience over two decades that of every
hundred students who come to me to learn computing—and
they are supposedly highly motivated and supposedly educated up to that point—there will be two or three who will
show promise of catching on to the art of computing. Three
percent or so will demonstrate to me that they have their
heads fastened on properly, and I can certify them to anyone
as possible good trainees and not cringe if they tell who
their teacher was. Three percent is pretty low, and I
haven't been able to increase it in twenty years, all aptitude
tests notwithstanding. That leaves a lot of students who get
a degree and who claim to have been exposed to computing,
but I wouldn't trust them near the master files if I were running a commercial installation.

Over the years, at these symposia, the question keeps coming up: What are you people in the academic world doing to supply personnel to handle the horrendous problems that we have? Usually, the only ones present to try to answer that question have been the professors from UCLA who happen to be here, and that isn't quite fair. So for this session, we rounded up what we think is the proper cross section: representatives from a two-year school, a four-year school, and a commercial school.

The teaching of computing is different from teaching other subjects, in many ways. Teachers of any subject sometimes fall into the trap of thinking that if they utter pearls of wisdom, the students will hear and understand them. That's fatuous, as every teacher knows. Usually they're not listening anyway; they're writing. But at least in computing, we have a mechanism for feedback over and above simple regurgitation. The students who learn go out and compute, and they can demonstrate and display their knowledge. The same thing could occur in a chemistry course, but the feedback might result in the loss of the chem lab.

Prof. Gerald

I greatly appreciate this opportunity for soul-searching. Analyzing our problems and developing alternatives for their solution is appropriate for all of us in the data processing industry. It is particularly appropriate for us educators because quality control on our product is most difficult to obtain. Teachers of computer science have an especially acute problem because there is no accepted definition for the term "computer science." Data processing conveys a more generally accepted image, but even here there is no real agreement.

Computer science education is characterized by a great variety of curricula, all of which seem to be different. At Cal Poly, we are probably more different than most. Our curriculum is largely self-manufactured. While Curriculum 68 is a popular model for building computer science curricula, we cannot claim other than a general resemblance to that pattern for education. This may be an advantage.

The general educational philosophy at Cal Poly, and one which dominates nearly every one of its programs, is to provide an occupationally centered and applications-oriented education. We mix professional education and general education courses throughout the whole four years. Our objective in doing this is to avoid the compartmentalization of much conventional college education. Since the professional man and the informed citizen are the same individual, his education in these two areas needs not only to overlap, but to be thoroughly integrated. Our departmental objectives also place emphasis on the applications of theory and avoid abstractions for their own sake.

Our program is a new one. Though we are only in our third year, we already have a significant number of faculty and student majors. We now have over 250 majors in the Bachelor of Science in Computer Science program, and next fall expect nearly 300. The 14 faculty members who teach computer science courses to these students also teach a number of courses to nonmajors as a service to our college community.

The required courses for a computer science major include what we call our core curriculum. Three courses in this core introduce the student to computer organization and assembler language programming. We treat computer organization in general terms, contrasting different examples from the spectrum of commercial computers, and also study IBM systems more intensively. A fourth course in data structures completes the groundwork that the student needs to go into his advanced sequences. These include a pair of courses in computer operating systems and another pair of courses that compare the features of higher-level languages as well as the compilers needed to provide these features. Especially pertinent to this discussion are the senior project and senior seminar courses. I shall discuss these in more detail a little later.

Paralleling these courses that provide the central core are a number of peripheral sequences. We try to give the student facility with a number of higher-level languages, and he uses them to program typical applications problems.

There are courses that develop the ability to use the computer as a model of business and scientific systems. There are courses in scientific computing through applied numerical analysis. The student elects courses in more specialized areas such as computer graphics and minicomputers. Fifteen percent of a student's graduation requirements are free electives, and he is encouraged to use these electives to adapt his program to his individual career objectives.

We define a computer scientist as one who is expert in computer systems and software, with a general knowledge of computer applications.

What we try to do at Cal Poly is also illustrated by what we don't attempt to do. We do not try to train applications experts within this program. Our feeling is that these persons should be centered in the area of applications and be knowledgeable about the use of the computer as a tool. In contrast, our majors are centered at the computer and look about them for areas they can serve. For example, we believe the best training for the business applications programmer is a major in business. We have developed, with our Business Administration Department, a management information systems concentration to train such business applications programmers. Similarly, there are computer science options in other application areas, developed jointly with them.

These applications-oriented programs will eventually produce at Cal Poly about an equal number of graduates who identify with the computer as our own computer science graduates. In addition, all of our engineering graduates have a working knowledge of computer programming. There is an increasing interest in our agricultural and social science areas in computers. Many of Cal Poly's architecture majors, numbering 1500 students, are using the computer as an interactive design tool. Computers and computer science play a major role in education at Cal Poly.

Because of the magnitude of these programs, we need to be acutely aware of the problems that we face. We have all the problems of education in general, which I think are to make education relevant to the student, closely related and illustrative of the real world, and a basis for solving the problems he will meet in later life. The newness of our discipline, the need to comprehend a rapidly growing technology, and insufficient resources to give students the exposure to computer systems that they should have, add to the burden of the educator. It is easy to fall into the trap of using simplistic examples and superficial exercises because of these problems.

Probably the first line of attack in solving any problem is to be aware that it exists. We hope that we have gone beyond that point of awareness in some of the things we do at Cal Poly. We try not to separate theory from practice. Theory is necessary, but in our opinion, only to help the student solve problems more effectively. We try to make the student aware of the magnitude of real problems though this is not easy to do. A real problem is usually too big and takes too long and requires too much computer resource to be assigned in most classes. I'm afraid we mostly point at the real problem and emphasize how small a subset is the actual exercise that has been assigned the student.

Good documentation is another important item that is hard to teach. We try to do it by integrating documentation into each and every course and certainly we never teach documentation as a separate topic. The problem here is related to the insignificance of the usual programming assignment. For example, who can be convinced that he should flowchart the simple exercise of the beginning COBOL course which reads a card and prints its image with only a slight rearrangement of the fields? Who needs a decision table to understand the logic of a FORTRAN program that adds three numbers?

Much of our effort at Cal Poly in preparing effective computing personnel finds its fruition in the senior project. Every graduate from Cal Poly, and certainly every graduate from the computer science curriculum, must execute a senior project. This is an individual effort of significant magnitude, in which he applies his prior knowledge. It combines the integration of his earlier coursework with the need to plan and execute a project under his own initiative. He does

this work under the guidance of a faculty member who as-
sumes the role of work supervisor in simulation of a future
professional assignment. Major emphasis is given on thorough documentation of the work and clarity and completeness
of its exposition in the written description. We have had
some outstanding performances already in the short time
that we have been producing computer science graduates.
One particularly noteworthy project had the title, "Educational Applications of Computers." Behind that title lies a
thoroughly developed information system whereby a teacher
could access student records, update these records, and
modify them at will. Because of the limitations of the college's computer facility, the student developed this in a
batch environment but except for that compromise, it was a
complete and workable management information system
oriented to the classroom teacher. We have had other outstanding demonstrations of the student's professional ability
to use the computer effectively.

Each graduate also has had a course called the senior
seminar. In this course there is great emphasis on the
development of communications skills. The student presents
significant topics from the current literature to his classmates as an individual presentation. He receives comments
from the class as well as his instructor in order to improve
this ability. He practices leading a group discussion and
participates in panel presentations. This course, which
stresses verbal communication, supplements the senior
project, which emphasizes written communications skills.

A significant percentage of our students also elect to do
a special project. These have varied widely and are usually
student-initiated projects in which the student applies the
computer in a way that is interesting to him, under the
guidance of one of our faculty members. Through regularly
scheduled conferences this faculty member advises the student on resources available and acts as a consultant to help
him over the hard spots. We have had students do everything from software development to applying the computer
in the solution of real problems in our college environment.

We are aware of special difficulties that we have at Cal

Poly in making our educational program even more effective. San Luis Obispo is remote from major centers of computing activity and large-scale users of computing machinery. This means that we do not have local experts that we could bring in as part-time teachers to expose our students to a variety of current real-world problems. Our faculty are painfully aware of their lack of continuing contacts with the computing industry. This geographical remoteness means that our students have little facility for part-time work experiences. Even though only a small number of students may be employed, they can bring their experience into the classroom and share it with their classmates. A significant number of our majors do find employment in the college's computer center, but we recognize that this is not a typical operation. We are exploring ways to overcome this problem.

We particularly desire to be effective in educating computer scientists beyond the Bachelor's level in our forthcoming Master of Science program. That program provides for a choice of two out of five parallel emphasis areas; by this choice a variety of career objectives can be served. We are incorporating what we think to be a unique experience, entitled "Computer Science Practicum." The Practicum comes after the sequences that develop graduate-level knowledge in the areas, and involves group attack on a real-world problem. We have asked a number of industrial firms to cooperate with us in developing the problems to be attacked during the Practicum. Their response has been enthusiastic and they seem willing to commit a significant amount of effort. One of their professionals will come to our campus to explain the problem to our students, and they will permit our students to visit their facility both at the beginning and at the end of the Practicum project. The students' first visit will be to discuss the project with a number of their technical people and to gain an idea of the environment in which this problem is embedded. At the end of the project the students will again travel to the participating company to make a formal presentation to their technical personnel. We feel that this Practicum will be the highlight of our Master's program.

Another important part of our Master's degree program is an intensive foundations course which will permit many students to enter the program in addition to those whose undergraduate training is in computer science or information science. We believe that strong business graduates, engineers, and scientists will contribute much when they sit in the classroom with graduates from undergraduate programs similar to ours. The foundations course is being developed to permit them to enter the professional-level courses with an adequate background.

Mr. Reynolds

Our college is one of two colleges in the Coast Community District. Ours started in 1947 and presently has over 18,000 full-time students. Computer studies began in 1958. We average some 900 students per year in the Business Information Systems curriculum. We are a focal point for visitation and examination by computer educational groups from all over the world. There are some 70 army personnel attending our college on military contract each year. We hold summer institutes for educators in computing, and seminars in computer-assisted learning for educators in many disciplines. We are now starting a TV-based open university program that will incorporate computers, telecommunications, audio/visual aids and other teaching devices.

The Coast Community Colleges operate an installation with a System 360/50 with a megabyte of slow core and 384K bytes of fast core, with two tape drives and 16 disk drives. The system supports 96 time-shared terminals and functions around the clock.

The college offers courses in all of the popular computer languages, including assembly language, FORTRAN, COBOL, RPG, PL/1 and APL. There are courses in Management Information Systems, Data Communication Systems, and Installation Management, as well as Computer Operations and Advanced Computer Software.

The underlying philosophy of the curriculum involves helping the student to think for himself; to understand his environment as interrelating, interdependent, dynamic systems.

Beyond our formal courses, there are arrangements for independent study for students who have the ability and motivation to pursue their own directions with a given area.

The mathematics department sponsors three courses in Computer Science which are well coordinated with our courses in Business Information Systems.

Aptitude is of tremendous importance, even though it is relatively scarce in the student ranks. In any case, there is a tremendous rise in the effectiveness of the student over the two-year period he is with us. Our graduates are in demand in local industry.

We have a work-experience program for any student who is employed in a computer-related area. In this program, the student, his employer, and the college sign an agreement that centers around the student's planned development on the job. A work-experience coordinator (a professor from the Business Information Systems department) works with the company and the student jointly and separately in order to help optimize the student's school studies in coordination with various learning experiences available on the job. We seem to be getting good results from this program.

My own specialty is in the systems area. Although we try to incorporate some systems perspective in all of our courses, the main emphasis is in tying it all together with the human being occupying every second link in the chain. The burden of this integration falls on the systems courses.

Many students are attracted to the program not only for the promise of monetary reward, but also for the promise of a hiding place from the rigors of a cruel society. The computer seems to offer an extension of their television set syndrome, whereby they can vicariously participate without having to face actual competition with live personalities. They are fascinated by the opportunity to crawl into a corner and solve problems with no one but an inanimate computer. As with the TV set, they are free to rant and scream, to walk away, to show disgust and contempt, and even to pull the plug if they want to be absolutely free; there is no need to worry about human interaction on a moment-to-moment basis. They feel free to maintain every whim or attitude that might

be called freaky by others, and, best of all, they look forward to getting paid well and achieving considerable distinction and prestige for donning this mantle of freedom.

For many of our students, then, there is a significant
gasp of dismay when it finally dawns on them that a job as
"programmer" is actually a job of systems analysis that
involves human interaction. Many of them eventually refute
this understanding and disavow their belief that a programmer
does anything but code.

Accordingly, we do our best, in the short two years we
have allocated to the job, to expose the student to the principles of programming logic from a number of different
approaches:

- To provide initial perspective on computer operations,
  operating systems, the dynamics and apparent directions of the technology, the computing industry, and
  the profession.

- To provide perspective on organization design theory,
  management theory, and the tools and techniques of
  systems analysis.

- To provide perspective on communications with one's
  self and with others (i. e., general semantics) as an
  indispensable factor in the human cybernetic system
  underlying any organizational computer system.

- To provide perspective on the human characteristics
  and motivations of top executives, with the objective
  of reducing some of the awe and mystique that would
  freeze initiative of thinking in this area.

- To provide motivation towards effective leadership in
  promoting sound computer-based management information systems in particular areas of operation.

- To provide perspective on the near-future effects
  that the computer will have on the human being living
  in the cyberculture.

Some of our most difficult students are those refugees

from industry who claim years of experience. They are quick
to explain that they are there simply to pick up the formality
of a degree. It is clear to them that what they are being
taught in the systems line is so much hokum, since in the company where they worked things were done just the opposite for
years, and therefore the college courses must have it all
wrong.

We also have difficulty with some of the managers from
local industry, who may have strange ways of using computers
and programmers, but who expect us to train up to their
standards.

We are proud of our high standing with the United States
Army. We train their enlisted people for the top computer-
based systems positions in their world-wide installations.
The maturity and motivation of these military students give
us a base for the quality of curriculum that has made our
college world famous for its scholastic output in this area.
The Pentagon wants to be sure that its people have some perspective on the total interrelationship of all systems, the relationships of cybernetic human organization design, communications, coordination, and synergy to the objectives of
running that computer. We are happy to oblige them in their
wants insofar as we are able in two short years. The spill-
over to our regular students is tremendously beneficial for
all concerned.

MANAGING THE SYSTEM:
EXECUTIVE PARTICIPATION
IN COMPUTER DESIGN AND OPERATION

TERRANCE HANOLD

President
The Pillsbury Company

I am flattered by the title attached to this excursion. It suggests that an executive may participate in computer design and operation. And it makes the extreme implication that he may even influence its management.

If an executive is defined as a noncomputer type boxed in an office with carpet, drapes, and his own Centrex number, then I can make the qualifying flight. But when the field is further limited to those executives who have constructively participated in information systems design and management, then I doubt that I can survive the cut. Our information systems people are glad to give me public credit for a larger role when it serves their private ends. But they take care to keep me off their turf at home.

In the realm of infosystems concepts, I have some ideas which they allow me to express. If these opinions agree with the prejudices they have already formed, they cheerfully give me credit for their invention. If we differ, their convenient deafness closes the colloquy. So my comments describe the concepts we share, tactfully omitting all credits for their creation. But you may assume an unspoken discount respecting my contribution to any successes. Credit I am free to claim for all disasters.

And we have had a few disasters. My letter of invitation

read: "When we laid out the program, we said we were looking for the successful case study." Obviously, the program chairman had suffered reversals and had lowered his sights before he came to me. But unfortunately the publicity for this conference had already been issued, and the reference to "responsible information processing" had already been made. Such are the risks that attend long-range planning.

Whether there is a successful case study in responsible information processing is an open question. Predictably, a firm that has such a treasure will never display it. Only those who have, by repeated failure, been made indifferent to contempt are likely to take the stage. In my case, there is nothing by way of denigration or disparagement that you can say to me that would be unfamiliar. So in the interest of time, please save your aspersions.

We are in full understanding, then, that this plain and painful recital out of stark experience is no success story. But it does come within the strict terms of the descriptive matter in the program. It does pertain to our "experience in resolving the problem of effective EDP usage." Nothing is said here of solving the problem—only of resolving it— which is quite another result.

INFOSYSTEMS TARGET CONCEPTS

To get hold of this subject, I am going to discuss some concepts. Both of us realize that this device is oftener used to avoid the subject than to attack it. Of course, this may be the consequence here. As a speaker, I am somewhat accident prone. But it is not my purpose.

Since I am fairly uninformed in this field, I will be quite learned at the beginning. When I get thoroughly over my head, I shall become scholarly. And if everything goes to pieces, I shall be totally abstruse, covering my retreat with a barrage of indecipherable equations.

The key to any function design is the purpose it is to serve. The computer function can serve a variety of purposes, each appropriately characterized by a different adjective. Two of these differing purposes are described by the terms "efficient" and "effective." Neither purpose is inherently superior to the other, except as the needs of the entity served by the function may be better served in one mode rather than in the other. Using broad categories for these descriptive terms, we can aim the computer function at three successive levels of corporate purpose:

1. At the efficient level

2. At the effective level

3. At the generative level

It may be designed to perform efficiently if it is directed solely toward the administrative process of collecting, recording, and reporting history in an accounting frame. It may be done efficiently because the work to be done and the conditions to be met are known in advance. Hence, the resources required may be defined and applied with precision, and the efficiency of resource use may be measured with the same precision.

The computer function may be designed to perform effectively if it is addressed to the costing, scheduling, formulating, controlling, sales analysis, and other supportive procedures which characterize operations. In this context there are many factors imprecisely measurable in advance and a fair number of unknowns with which the computer function must deal. Thus, if the function is to satisfy the critical needs of operations at periods of peak demands, the system must have a reserve of excess resources. So the test of performance here is not the rate of utilization of resources, but the effectiveness of the supporting services supplied to operations. These may usually be measured or estimated independently of the performance level of the operations supported.

At the third level the computer function may be dedicated to a generative or executive purpose. The essential executive contribution is to generate change to advance the interests of the firm. Computer capabilities both complement and amplify the processes inherent in the executive function. They are more than supportive in nature. They are themselves instruments of change. When directed in this fashion, the separate measure of the efficient use or even of the effective use of computer resources is an impossible and irrelevant effort. When put to this use, it becomes an inherent part of the essential executive or generative process. Only a valuation of the change resulting from the whole process has meaning, with perhaps some estimate of the degree to which the infosystem clarified, expedited, or enlarged the result.

The number and nature of these options is not the product of a mystical revelation. Instead, they have become known to us by punishing degrees over a dozen years. Nor did we by instinct pick the right path at the outset and pursue it with entire devotion. Only as our knowledge has developed has our reach extended and our concept of the infosystems function enlarged.

A critical condition to growth in the infosystems function beyond the first stage is the quality of the firm's line and executive management. Only as their quality is tested and proved can the computer function grow through these successive stages to the generative level.

DESIGN TARGET REWARDS

While infosystems people are large-spirited by instinct and made almost oblivious to matters of compensation by the adventures of their calling, some estimate of the relative rewards offered by these alternative levels of function is a pertinent consideration.

Operating efficiently yields the maximum psychological reward to the professional staff, plus a thin commendation · from the controller. Operating effectively calls for considerable sacrifice of pure principle, but it does create a great reputation for productivity with the line management and a generally higher monetary reward. Operating executively offers little psychological income, earns no more than a skeptical regard at the line level, but obtains a uniformly sympathetic hearing at the annual planning conference and the largest obtainable budget.

Operating executively does have a deleterious effect on character. It generates a cynicism best expressed by one of our senior systems scientists at the start of our last

schematic development meeting, thus: "Okay, chief, so
we'll forget the harebrained idea you've had us chasing for
the last three weeks. What new, impossible delusion have
you dreamed up for our next all-out effort?"

When operating at the merely efficient level, computer
people occasionally suspect that those in the front office
have feet of clay. But when working generatively, they begin to surmise that their heads may be of the same material. Of course, this is demonstrable error. One can make
an impression on clay, at least until it is somewhat baked.

Nevertheless, we undertake to operate our information
system executively. As such, I think it satisfactorily serves
our needs at almost every level, including the administrative
and the operative stages. I do not expand that assessment to
declare that it successfully serves them. Satisfaction and
success are not necessarily congruent states. Indeed, in
the information field they must be infrequently and randomly
so. It is satisfactory because it does the best job possible
under the conditions that association with the executive side
imposes. Those conditions make a fully successful operation not merely unlikely, but totally incredible.

IN THE BEGINNING

Heaven is not gained at a single bound. Nor did we function in the executive mode from the start. To be blushingly
plain, we took off in 1958 in the evangelistic mode. We
moved our grocery division invoicing and receivables from
tab to tube with only 24 hours of parallel processing. We
were under the impression we would automate the entire
corporation the next weekend.

During the 18 months following, while we strove desper-
ately to reconstruct the books and to restore some semblance of a two-way cash flow, we formed the conviction
that the instant transfiguration of the data world was an impractical objective. By the close of 1959, we had had
enough of carping bookkeepers and they of us. That the accounting chores had to be done was certainly brought home
to us. But that there were other, and perhaps more important, areas of computer application beyond the administrative
was also dimly perceived.

When we faced the transistor age in 1962, we had re-
formed our ranks and reordered our priorities. We had decided to build from the bottom and to rise laboriously rung
by rung from the dusty earth of data processing to the vault-
ing skies of information systems. Some of you who missed
that trip may find this shift in course hilarious. But as
Henry V observed, they laugh at scars who never felt a
wound.

Our view of an information system was perfectly obscure.
What it was and how we were to get there were equally unde-
fined. But we were certain of a few things. It required an
immense centralized on-line data base; it required a com-
puter-managed communication system to make the data base
accessible to all data-generating-and-using points in the
firm; and it required as large a main frame as our business
could sustain to exploit the potential of the system.

These were our base lines. For our action plan we organized ourselves to attack three objectives. We laid out a
program to surround the administrative-level function as
our first project; we outlined a scheme to blueprint line support systems for the operative level as our second task; and
we promulgated ground rules that would keep our options
open respecting the future shape of the executive-level information system when its proper form and nature should be
revealed to us. In main part those ground rules were that:

1. No computer or computer-related services or equipment could be leased or purchased without the concur-
   rence of the head of corporate infosystems.

2. All systems must be centralized or capable of transfer to the central system.

3. All computer professionals must be either operation-
   ally or functionally responsible to the head of corporate infosystems.

In the course of the development process I have described
we began to see things in the round. Of course, yesterday's
transactions must be recorded, but today's line operations
must also be supported, and further, the executive

management must be armed against tomorrow. Computer contribution at the executive level was at that point a distant prospect, but it was the ultimate challenge.

It is true that line management is where the action is, where today is lived, and where support is sought. Yet the largest need was with the corporate executive who is accountable for the past, who is obliged to monitor the present, although he lacks the means of directing it, but whose greatest and driving responsibility is for the future.

We had from the beginning a clear enough idea of the means by which history could be recorded and reported. We could sketch out a rough scheme, good enough for a first step, of the systems required to support the line operations. But a blueprint for dealing with tomorrow wasn't included in our Ramac's software manual. If you ask your corporate management what they need to deal with tomorrow, you will get a quick answer--the power of divination and the gift of prophecy. But it isn't a readily useful answer.

We believed then, and are convinced now, that infosystems are the essential means by which executive management can meet these responsibilities. No resource aside from clairvoyance, which is not yet commercially available, can approach a data base indicative of the range of events possible of happening tomorrow, coupled with the means of estimating their probability or order of occurrence, or of simulating the shape which the corporation or the market will take upon their impact.

THE LONG MARCH

The core purposes of computer systems directed toward the administrative mode, and of most applications at the operative level, are to enlarge and accelerate data flows and to improve by advanced rationalization the impact of these data flows on the management of the current business. At least those were the purposes which guided us.

And we accomplished in these areas essentially what we intended. But we achieved more by accident than by design. At least it can be respectively argued that the by-products were of greater import than those proposed.

As an instance, the objectives served by the guides or controls described a few minutes ago were ruggedly simple. We intended to get the most computing power we could afford, and obviously we could get more bang per buck from one large system than from several small machines. We also intended to get more expertise by attracting more specialists at higher levels of capability rather than a crowd of generalists at lower levels of competence. We got these results with some unforeseen additions.

Suppliers are far more inclined to put their major resources against major systems where their use will result in development, rather than against a stable of smaller systems where the likely result is simple maintenance. And the inclination to extend support to major systems varies according to the quality of the user's staff. Suppliers grab ideas as well as give them.

Our infoservices staff has expanded by several magnitudes in the last decade, from a scatter of technicians to a battalion of highly trained professionals of several disciplines and specialties, of exalted status and with unimaginable perquisites and emoluments. And they are worth every dollar they receive. Or so I represent to a skeptical board of directors.

Their area of operation was once safely circumscribed by a glass wall, where they were caged with their computer. These confines are gone. They are now to be found in every administrative, marketing, production, research, sales, and planning group in every division and subsidiary of our firm. Corporately they represent one of the five indispensable consultative and analytical resources of the executive office.

In title, they are elevated and enlarged from EDP to Infoservices. The change in title is the product of a constantly expanding concept of their function. Organizationally, in ten years their function has moved from an adjunct of the systems department to an arm of the controller's function and then to an ally of the executive office, to which the head of infoservices directly reports.

Electronic data processing obtained entry into the business enterprise with the promise of cost reduction. In the interest of efficiency, we replaced clerical routines with first-generation EDP equipment. With the object of improving the effective use of data, we used communications computers to concentrate branch operations at a corporate center. Then to avoid the expense of repetitive handling of data at ascending levels in the administrative pyramid, our second-generation computers were used to chain the vertical links into a continuous processing system.

By the time our third-generation computer was on scene, several consequences, and I define a consequence as an unintended result, had followed from these efforts.

First, business data was converted from an exclusive property of the accounting department to a resource more universally available and directly accessible to each who had a claim on it.

Next, it created in and around the computer department a new area of competence within the corporation, staffed by a rapidly growing group of people of advanced skills of high order. Their entry into the corporate body fostered the entry or expansion of other personnel with advanced academic, technical, and professional qualifications in a wide range of corporate activities.

Third, these developments were accompanied by the continuous introduction of ever more, ever larger, and ever more sophisticated machinery to handle the immensely expanding data and decisional processing framework which supported these new groups.

Fourth, to improve the cost value ratio of the vast files which this system accumulated, management learned to submit to linear and simulative mathematical techniques which recover the fine gold of insight from the dross of data. Having by this experience been persuaded that there are values as well as costs in real data, the savants are now trying to persuade us of the usefulness of assumed data. And they have made some headway with their pitch. But certain of the management are still hesitant about losing themselves in a Bayesian forest of decision trees.

And there have been other consequences which have fundamentally altered between the structure of the corporation and the nature (or even the good nature) of its management.

Thus, when we merged 33 branch accounting operations of our Grocery Products Company into one rather small office in Minneapolis, we awoke to the fact that computer processes give the administrative manager an immediate horizontal reach over an incredibly enlarged direction span.

When we consolidated the successive steps in the data reporting pyramid, we discovered the compacting effect on organization of more advanced computer programming and the direct vertical reach to the theatre of action which it gave to the operations manager.

As computer operations expanded the manager's field of command, we were concerned whether the enlargement of his sphere would dilute the effectiveness of his direction. But a survey of the new world showed him to be more thoroughly in charge than he had been before.

At that point we began to appreciate the disciplinary results of electronic processes both in rationalizing our procedures and in enforcing the standards and controls built into our programs. A manager may now count on a quality of compliance with his plans and policies on the administrative side that is far superior to that given him by any supporting staff in the past.

Another immediate effect of computerization was the removal of a very large administrative function from the district sales manager and of a very large administrative supervisory job from his superior. This same process is taking place in the production and financial areas of the firm. All levels of management have been relieved of a substantial administrative burden, and of a multitude of recurring simple-choice operating decisions as well, which have been provided for in programmed routines.

Hence, all levels of management are able to address themselves more consistently and in a more professional manner to the conduct of the business which they are charged with prosecuting. All levels of management have access to current data, identical in content, describing the present state of things, as well as to an immense body of historical data.

Since through the use of planning models, he now sees his own activity in the perspective of all related operations, we

require a manager to be both specifically responsible within his own area and widely contributive to the areas that his
actions affect.

All levels of management have an increasing stock of
electronic and mathematical tools, many in a time-shared
remote-access mode, for the assembly, classification,
transmission, analysis, evaluation, and projection of banked
data—both to solve present problems and to forecast future
conditions.

The performance of each level of management is subject
on a current basis, because of the current data available to
the superior, to measurement and appraisal. This feature
of a computerized information system is not always appreciated as an advantage by a manager under review.

But the fundamental consequence of this condition has
been to the advantage of the operating management. So long
as the executive office was exposed only to fragmentary
historical data coming 30 to 45 days after the event, the
corporate executives were compelled to involve themselves
in operations to maintain a feel of the state and direction of
the business. Now that current data is fully available, reflecting the present state of affairs in main outline, the executive officers have largely withdrawn from operations in
order to pursue with more constant attention their proper
functions.

These are, of course, the development of general policy
for the guidance of the business, the study of the longer-
term goals of the firm, the planning of the forward growth
of the business, the definition of the range and mix of the
product lines for the coming years, the provision and allo-
cation of the resources that these plans will require, and
the development and measurement of operating management,
to name a few.

While the management information system has added to
the status of operating management and has put executive
management in its proper place, what has been the fate of
middle management in a computerized environment? The
predictions of the fate of middle management have been dire,
and, in our experience, unfounded. They were based on the
assumption that middle management's function must be

administrative—to control clerical routines, to transmit and execute operating management's directions.

In fact, middle management has steadily grown as a proportion of our salaried staff since 1960, and my belief is that as computerization proceeds, their proportion will at least hold and may grow further. The reason for the survival and increase of middle management lies in its shift in function from the routine supervision of people to the management of much of the business.

Modern information systems have multiplied the data relevant to management decisions as well as the tools for putting it to work in the decisional process. Data reflecting the living present is opportunity. Its vast increase as we reach into current time systems has opened the way to the involvement of many more brains and talents, of many more disciplines and technologies, to mine the profits it enfolds. And since data values are ephemeral, most of the decisions must be made by the middle manager—there is not time to pass the buck to the division manager.

How does middle management operate? It does not run itself according to the organization chart. The box and line structure is almost irrelevant, except for purposes of status, to an operating business organization. The box and line chart was built on the flow of information up, of directions down, and of reports back. The flow is not that way anymore. The main direction middle management receives is from the information system, not from the general management. Middle managers must be self-generating people.

While this is not all I have on the subject, it is enough to demonstrate that infosystems are inherently change mechanisms and that they operate powerfully in that fashion even when they are totally directed toward administrative and operative ends. Certainly, the evidence legitimizes the objective of merging them in straightforward fashion into the executive change mechanism.

WHY ARE WE HERE?

At about this junction people are inclined to inquire: Why are you involved? Why don't you go home and let computer people run computers? The answer is pretty clear. I regard computers and the structures we build on them as much too important to leave to computer people.

The business corporation, like most dynamic institutions in our society, is characterized by growth in transactions and resources at a compounding rate and by growth in diversity and complexity at an exponential rate. Because of the multiplying skills required and the diminishing reaction times allowed in the competitive arena, the corporate executive has no more than a disappearing chance of actually running the business.

His dilemma is that he has escalating responsibilities for the whole show and declining power to perform, or even to get onstage, in his own person. Unless he finds a means of setting the stage in advance so as to assure in substantial degree the success of the enterprise, he is not at all in charge. He is simply the fall guy. Infosystems had to be one of his best means of planning and guiding the business, without its actual management and direction. And this is about his only means of monitoring the action as it goes on.

Thus, the corporate executive must be keenly interested in the shape taken by the key infosystems. Either his ideas will shape them, or they will from that time forward shape his course of action.

Does this mean centralized control of the business by computer-enforced restraints? Quite the opposite. A centralized infosystem is the prime resource for a successfully decentralized firm. We work extremely hard to that end because we believe in that route to profit and expansion. To foster the ability of our divisions to leave home without leaving the infosystem, we have just finished the formidable job of putting a highly computerized $200 million business totally on a remote-access basis. It can now operate with equal facility 10 feet or 2000 miles from headquarters.

The corporate safeguard is that we know the data base and the systems theory on which they work; and just as they have access to the main data base, so central systems has access to all of the data generating and storage points in that division. In these circumstances, it is easy to understand their plans, it is easy for them to incorporate our goals and guides, and monitoring performance by each of us in the same context is automatic.

Similarly, we are in the process of blending an acquired subsidiary's communication system into the corporate system and placing some of its data base in the central data base. As this process develops, mutual understanding comes faster and easier.

We are just beginning a truly mammoth project, motivated by the rapid growth in food technology and governmental directives respecting food safety, to provide an integrative mechanism for the entire materials handling and processing flow from commodity to consumer product. It will link R and D, procurement, transportation, manufacturing, quality assurance, warehousing, and distribution. The company has a big stake in this, and I have a critical personal interest as well.

So I have a fundamentally different point of view from that which you have expressed. You are looking at a business in its fragments on a man-by-man basis and inquiring what each wants in the way of data and reports. I am looking at the whole business and saying that this tool, if I use it well, permits me to shape the organization as I want it, to provide the data basis which I think is necessary for business intelligence and decision, to furnish analytical and predictive tools that I think are credible in result, and to supply the communication language and link by which the businesses and the corporation maintain liaison.

An infosystem is a regenerative interactive system. A computer program is simply an input-output production facility. I am concerned with systems which manage a flow of information, not with the static product of a piece of the system. The format of a report is critical to the mind that doesn't understand its meaning. At worst it is an incidental irritation to the mind that is intent on the action that the report can generate.

As I remarked earlier, the use of infosystems in the executive mode is dependent on the management climate, or in the words of today, is governed by the environment. Does the management environment foster or frustrate the exploitation of computer-based functions as a system?

There is an established attitude in managements that rejects involvement with mathematical concepts, and, of course, a computer is mathematics in a material form. There is the ineradicable inclination to fly by the seat of the pants, a generally unfounded regard for "hunch" under the facade of "experienced judgment."

To counter this, our best results have been obtained through high-level seminars on decision systems, on financial analyses, on sales planning and forecasting, where the computer is seemingly quite subordinate in its role. But we get involvement by providing problems using timesharing terminals for their solution, problems which permit multiple results which encourage repeated runs in the search for more optimal results.

Because we did some developmental work in the field when time-sharing was an infant, we now have a generally established tradition of acceptance of systematic thinking in matters of organization, planning, and problem solving. The climate, consequently, for the exploitation of infosystems at the executive level is first rate.

We have always kept in sight a larger purpose than that justified by our immediate plans and programs. When people establish efficiency or effectiveness as the measures of their goals, our experience says that they raise constraints against larger accomplishments. We have always invested seed money toward more distant ends, for if we fail in this we shall fall short of those ends when they become possible of attainment. We believe that we will always lag our potential if we limit our objectives to those which the immediately emerging state of the art will support.

As an example, we invested in time-sharing three or four years in advance of the time when in-house equipment could support it. For another, we started the design and infrastructure of an integrated data base at least five years ago. Today, when the equipment that can truly support it is at last on site, we have a satisfactorily operative system on stream. Such is the rapidity of advance in the computer art that the most forehanded efforts do no more than keep us current in utilizing capability gains.

We intend to proceed effectively, and on our better days efficiently, against a succession of limited objectives. Of course, accomplishment is achieved only if effort is applied within severely defined limits. But these limited objectives are selected and related by their order of support for larger purposes usually beyond present capability. So our course has been one of successive specific achievements within the frame of a constantly enlarging purpose.

This philosophy probably contradicts good engineering practice, and it isn't particularly congenial to systems analysis people, but I think it is first-rate management direction in a high-risk, high-return area, all of whose dimensions are unknown. By these means we hope to avoid the mismatch of "introducing fourth-generation computers, while still exploiting the possibilities of third-generation computers, using second-generation computer management concepts." (Conference Board Record, March 1972, page 27)

DATA PROCESSING'S HIGHER RESPONSIBILITIES

ALAN TAYLOR, MSCDP

President
The Society of Certified Data Processors

"The challenge to the computer community is clear--they must creatively ensure that people, not paper, are important." These were some very courageous words written by a Californian, Mr. Dee Hock, President of National Bank-Americard. They were courageous because Mr. Hock, in order to make his points, had to outline a series of reasons for believing that data processors had not given due respect to people. Unlike ourselves, Mr. Hock was not in a position to cite references from computer manuals, or from meetings about special interest groups, and so he had to rely upon the experiences—the bad experiences—within his own organization. In fact, he had to practically admit that his operation had failed the people that they were supposed to serve in order to make his case against the data processing profession.

He did it, for which we must be truly thankful. For we must admit that it is a higher degree of courage than that exhibited elsewhere in our profession. A more typical attitude was shown in January this year when the leader-writer of Computer Weekly, a major trade newspaper in Great Britain, commented that the question of what is—or is not— good practice is not one that interests either the public or the members of the profession, in England or in the USA. The comment came as the British Computer Society was preparing to rush into publication a so-called agreed code of good practice with less than two months between the date of

146

its publication and the one and only public consideration of it.

More to the point, having claimed that there was so little professional or public interest in the matter, the leader-writer used this contention to defend the action of the British Computer Society, saying that any code is better than none.

Factually, of course, he is not correct. Recent actions by Consumers Union, by Mr. Hock, by the editors of Amer-ican Banker, and by others show that the public is now much more interested than they ever were. Within the profession, the actions of my own society, the Society of Certified Data Processors, and the results of the general polls which have been taken both through the Society and through the use of the Society-sponsored Professional Viewpoint Page in Com-puterworld have shown that the profession also is waking up from a long era of apathy. So does the ACM Ombudsman program, and the recent Time/AFIPS survey on the public attitude toward computers.

But along with these evidences of increasing public con-cern we must also face up to a record of computer failure, and computer people's failure. The Time/AFIPS survey showed that tens of millions of people have had trouble with their computers, and their various billing systems. My correspondence shows that this does not exist simply among the ignorant, or the uninformed, but instead is rampant in the profession and outside it. Recently, when I was talking on this subject to the Joint DPMA Chapters of the Greater Cleveland area, the microphone was besieged by people standing up and telling of their problems. One letter subse-quently told me of one company who responded—eventually— to a computer problem by sending out a check so that the recipient could send it in and thereby clear an erroneous computer balance! Is this the way we should be dealing with matters? I think not.

Nor can I recommend that method adopted by the Internal Revenue Service. Their technique in order to obtain the use of computers in making their tax audits has been to outlaw the idea of keeping records in hard-copy form. They do not find it sufficient anymore—if you do happen to be putting them on a computer. So far they have not demanded that they all go on computers.

The law, of course, does permit the IRS to demand that adequate records are kept, and does allow the IRS to define what documents constitute adequate records. Whether or not this permits the IRS to outlaw hard copy appears, to say the least of it, to be dubious. However, the IRS has made that point rather moot by simply creating a ruling (71/20) which says that records maintained on punch cards, magnetic tapes, or magnetic disks are records within the meaning of the IRS law, and must therefore be retained indefinitely.

They have told the Society of Certified Data Processors that this does mean that if any accounting data is used and temporarily placed upon any tape or disk, then unless the IRS agrees otherwise (at conferences which they have proposed to hold annually), the taxpayer must retain the media involved.

They also admit that retention of every tape and disk would be economically punitive, but say that such broad powers are needed so as to prevent hard copy from being able to be regarded as being adequate records.

I cannot say that I think much of this form of argument, but I am even more disturbed by the failure of the IRS to understand data processing adequately enough to realize what they have done. In the first case they have asked for a technical impossibility. How shall we run a sort on accounting data without reusing our scratch tapes? How shall we place data upon a disk built in to a computer system before retrieval and moving onto a disk pack, or tapes, without allowing it to be over-written later? And how shall we make available for inspection a built-in disk which we ourselves cannot inspect?

What they have asked is technically foolish, and impossible—unless we take it in another way. The actual noun in the sentence says that the medium is what has to be preserved. It says nothing whatsoever about the recordings on it. It would appear, therefore, that a computer installation would be perfectly within its rights simply to note the tape number, or the disk number that the data was on and say to the inspectors "This is the reel on which we put some accounting data on March 16th, 1972. Of course it now holds a program for creating electronic music—but all you asked for was the medium to be preserved, not the recording!"

This is the type of technical standard for laws and regulations which will be coming to regulate data processing if they are brought from outside, and if we within the profession do not look to see what the problems are. For the fact is that while the Chairman of the Board of IBM, Mr. Vincent Learson, may happily write in Datamation that he has no trouble with computer people, because he is one, the world is having trouble with data processing and we must realize it, and respond to it if we are to fulfill our higher responsibilities.

As a first measure, therefore, we must look for the failures and see what has happened that should not have happened. It is often worthwhile looking around in our own backyards before we go out into the great world. It often gives us clues as to where the problems have arisen. We currently speak in a technical/university environment. Very well then, let us look at some of the results that have been obtained by technical/university environments. And let us look at how they have affected the operations of the ordinary computer user.

In 1964 there was introduced an extremely powerful set of computers. These were technically extremely flexible because most of them were microcoded. Microcoding, of course, was a well-known art, particularly in this part of the world with Packard Bell's 250 and 440, and with Standard Computer systems shortly thereafter. Even earlier, in the late 1950's, the Stantec Zebra had offered programmers some of the same capabilities. And yet it was not until 1968, four years later, that the ACM Special Interest Group on microprogramming held its first conference. The conference was not open. People who were not employed at microprogramming were not allowed into it. Apparently it would imperil the right of academic freedom to open it. The reason that this infringement would occur would be because the companies who employed the microprogrammers would order them not to say anything, and would perhaps take them

out of the system. This was successful in preventing the
spread of news of microprogramming.

Just how important this was did not become clear until
recently when we could see how little microprogramming
had been used, how much it could have been used, and what
the results were. Microprogramming had been used to
change the performance of one public Model 50, that of a
time-sharing service in California. It could have been used
to have improved the performance of all the systems by up
to 11.8 times! This was known to IBM in a specialized
study, which was published in Samir S. Husson's book,
Micro-programming Principles and Practices, in 1970.
But by 1970 the marketing needs of the firms had changed.
Now the idea was not to ask people to get the most out of
their computers, but instead to buy new ones. And so the
innate efficiencies of microprogramming were kept con-
cealed throughout a generation, computer programs were
charged, based on time, up to 10 times more than they need
have been, and now more than a billion dollars' worth of
perfectly good equipment is being obsoleted.

It is being obsoleted not becase the university/technical
community did not know of the capabilities of the system,
but because they did not dare protest the operations of the
marketing forces involved in their industry. They did not
dare challenge the claim of the Chairman of the Board of
IBM that he was, in fact, a technical person and a member
of the "computer community." It is one of our first responsibilities to accept the fact that while he may be a rich uncle,
and while we may be greatly dependent for our salaries upon
the computer manufacturers, they are not a part of the data
processors—they are merely a service organization, and
should be treated as such.

In another instance the university/technical community
was involved in a study estimating the future of data processing by a technique called "the Delphi technique." Many
people believe greatly in this technique; others are inclined
to refer to it as "group grope." I am not at this moment
prepared to pass any judgment on this.

When the results came in, they included a message of
very considerable significance to both the labor movement

and the politicians. It occurred when they started estimating just when superhuman capabilities would be available in computers so computers could replace people in factories. The estimate came distressingly soon. Indeed, the estimates showed that this was expected to have happened already within two presidential administrations.

That naturally suggests that labor, and the country, should be planning for such replacement. The types of labor and political leaders who were selected by one of our major technical user groups, by IBM's central planning areas, and by the university professor who chaired the whole operation also saw the need for such national interest. And so they brought it out in a diagram. This shows that the type of interest they expected was that the nation should, through tax incentives, assist in paying for the replacement of employees out of factories!

I wonder if the labor movement would agree. And I wonder whether academic freedom prevented access to this extremely important result. (Incidentally, just how carefully such secrets are actually guarded may be seen by the fact that a year later it did appear, unexpurgated, in another university publication which did not even bother to put a copyright notice on it!)

It is, therefore, one of our higher responsibilities that when results appear which indicate that government, or such important segments of the nation as the labor movement, are involved, the data processing professional has a responsibility to see that the news is open for evaluation.

In the past, in the same way that we have failed our employers by not insisting that the providers of computers allow us to use them thoroughly, we have also failed our nation by not warning them loudly and clearly of the potential of ideas that are close at hand.

When we have such failures, how can we possibly expect to respond thoroughly to Mr. Dee Hock's challenge that we make people, not paper, important? How can we possibly call ourselves professionals unless we are referring to the professional whose color is red, rather than a more progressive type?

The answer is that we cannot. The world-wide failure—
I did not bring in the British operation out of pure accident
—indicates that the system that we are working under is
wrong. It indicates that there is something in this current
system which prevents our operating on these true professional levels.

A moment ago I referred to the professionals whose col-
or is red. Coming from Massachusetts, I am also aware
of some other professionals—we might call them professional martyrs—who are so fixed that their color is in the
blue laws at the other end of the spectrum.

Indeed, you can create a whole spectrum of professionalism, including those who are so frightened that they are
not prepared to do anything—their color is yellow, of
course—and those who, while understanding the ideals,
still have a certain amount of caution and so mix both the
blue and yellow and come up with the progressive green.
When I refer to professionalism, it is those who can be
colored green that I am talking about.

It is quite clear from the history of the past 20 years
that the data processing profession has not yet matured. I
think it is up to us to discover how to mature. The Society
of Certified Data Processors has started—in response to
the challenge of Mr. Hock—a serious look at the structure
of our industry, our professional bodies, the way we program, the way we report, the way we are paid, and other
matters, for the purpose of discovering just what it is within the structure of the profession which is preventing us
from being professionals. My invitation to you individually
is to assist us in such a study, or to provide one of your
own. This is a necessary prerequisite before we can attempt to consider the high duties. We must first of all find
the fundamental sins.

And in parallel with this, the Society is also asking for
employers who bear the responsibilities of computers, and
who have permitted the use of equipment, although they
know that it is not warranted to be suitable for the task, and
have demanded the use of software, although they know that
there may be hundreds of flaws with it, to provide and demand the professional environment which will allow us to

make people more important than paper. If we have the resources, I would like to see the Society go further. I would like to see it consider the problems involved in the fact pointed out by the leader-writer of Computer Weekly: that generally the public is apathetic. Despite the evidence, they will apparently not raise complaints, and let whatever comes come. To some extent this may be beyond us—because it may mean that the public simply has the sense to believe that it does not matter what they think, or how they are treated, they will not be able to have anything changed. But even if this is so, and I hope that it is not, then we should know what the situation is, know how the profession can effectively speak, how often we have to talk and whom we have to talk to—to bring out the realities that are coming, and so help the world to be prepared for them, or even—where necessary—to prevent their coming into being. Such a study is also one of the higher responsibilities of the data processing professional.

There are others—naturally. There is the one which relates the duty we owe to our employers to the funding that is necessary for the various studies. If, after all, a billion dollars worth of equipment is currently going into obsolescence because its owners are still, after eight years, not able to use it as powerfully as it is capable of being used, then there is a source of savings here for our employers. It may be possible to arrange that these savings are made available to assist and protect those employers from the plagues of computer mistakes that we have, and from unprofessional behavior in general. This would then provide us with the funds for becoming professionals, including the funds for doing some of the more unpopular studies.

I do not know the answers. I will be listening very carefully to any suggestions that anyone puts forward. But I assure you most solemnly that unless our profession finds the answers, and finds them quickly, we will not merely be the scapegoats for the failures of the future, we may also be their cause.